Portals of Life

a process to

LIGHT, INSIGHT, FOCUS, EMPOWERMENT

JUDI WEISBART

ISBN: 0615764754
ISBN13: 9780615764757
Library of Congress Control Number: 2013902193
Judi Weisbart
Santa Barbara, CA

THIS BOOK IS DEDICATED TO:

MY HUSBAND, Harry, the **Light** in my life, my mother, Sheila for her loving **Insight** and support, my son, Adam for the **Focus** his birth created in me and the amazing love he brought into my life and my step-children and grandson for the **Empowerment** that they embody in all they do in the world.

LIFE is the greatest gift of all.

I have received so many gifts in this life from my mentors, friends and family including the Angels, Brian Ehrman, Cara Tilston, Kathy Winter, Patti Marcus, Sara Miller McCune, Sue Colin, the Tribe, Women's Executive Network and Yoel & Eva Haller.

I begin this book with gratitude to all for their many gifts.

Table of Contents

The Portals of Life can be studied with the
author weekly thru her online webinars.
Check for available times and days at
www.theportalsoflife.com

The Introduction & Inspiration for the Portals of LIFE

NEARLY THREE HUNDRED YEARS AGO Benjamin Franklin compiled a list of thirteen words or virtues he believed would contribute to his happiness and success. Each week he would focus on one virtue and its meaning and put into practice as he went about his daily life. Franklin believed that by repeating the cycle four times a year his mind would be taught a systematic way to think about these issues with purpose and intention and would bring about a keen sense of priorities, values, ideas, and the meaning of life. I have come to refer to his thirteen principles of "Ben's Wisdoms" or often referred to as "Ben's Virtues"

I began practicing Ben's Wisdoms more than eighteen years ago when I taught a weekly class on entrepreneurship and business planning in weekly meetings with a group of women through a nonprofit organization called Women's Economic Ventures (WEV) in Santa Barbara, California. The teaching process was difficult for a variety of reasons not the least of which was the fact that the average age of my students was 40 and most of them had not seen the inside of a classroom in twenty years or more.

I knew they would need to develop great focus and clarity to learn how to write a business plan so I assigned "Ben's Wisdom" to help them with their thought processes. As a homework assignment my students would write in their journals about issues in their life and how Ben's principles impacted their perceptions of their families, their communities and society at large. The weekly classroom conversation that followed their writing exercises proved enlightening and quite profound.

My teaching experience with "Ben's Wisdom" inspired me to create a new millennium version for people who want to work on their lives and identify their priorities and values. Thus was born the Portals of LIFE. Life is an acronym for light, insight, focus and empowerment. These four words represent the entire process. When the **light** of knowledge goes off in your head it gives you **insight** into your self and the world. Once inside it becomes the **focus** and the strength that you need to create **empowerment** in your LIFE.

The Portals of LIFE is a twenty-six week journey toward self-discovery that is embarked upon twice a year. It is the road map for life travelers, masters of destiny, the wise and the wannabe's.

This book has many layers and meanings, including the title itself. As I envisioned the work we could accomplish with such a process the idea of "one door closing and another opens" gave me a reassuring sense of LIFE. Even when one loses a job or a friend ultimately another job, friend or experience is about to enter your life. It is both exciting and frightening. What kind of job is out there for me? Will I be good enough? Will another person really want to be my friend? How can I trust that this is the right person? We all have doubts and fears but what I have learned is that those are just moments of growth and ultimately become the strength in our lives.

So as we begin this journey you will open and close doors, gates, and windows from around the world. As we venture forth thru these portals more gifts will be revealed to you. The photographs have been compiled from my travels to Europe, South America, India, China and the United States. As you consciously begin the process please spend a few moments thinking about the thousands of others who have stepped thru these portals and then begin the journey.

As you prepare for the journey remember to do the work. Use a journal to write it all down and look inside and outside for the answers, perspectives, and meaning to the word and virtue of the week. However, like all journeys you must take the first step, you have to do the work, read the word of the week every day, write in your journal for fifteen minutes each day and answer one of the questions that corresponds with the word. The best practice of the process is to first create a dedicated workspace and choose a regular time in the day when you are able to focus without interruption or distraction. You will want to visit bookstores, libraries or go online and download books to a reading device or pick up the reading suggested in each chapter or find something else on the subject that grabs your attention. Feel free to select other materials in addition to the suggested books listed at the end of each chapter. It might be a good idea for you to put together a group of like-minded people to meet and talk about significant words each week. Everyone will have a different perspective and the conversation will have a special value to each of the individuals participating. This is a time to look within yourself and into the words for the answers, perspective and meaning each week. Listen to your inner wisdom as it has much to say.

The most important aspect of the process is to maintain an open mind and give freedom to your thoughts. Remember the purpose of the exercise is to learn who you are and who you want to become as Benjamin Franklin did hundreds of years ago. This book and the process will help you to use your mind in a constructive way, to make real your vision of life and to imagine the life that you want to see.

The understanding of the process of The Portals of LIFE

Benjamin Franklin was my inspiration for this book but my work on this book was my final understanding of one of my life's purposes. I needed to write this so I could learn it. I needed to finish this so I could feel complete. It has been an interesting journey and I hope the readers find this process as fun and demanding as I have.

This book is not a place to just receive information. It is the place to be inspired to find it! Please find your way to learn more about this amazing man and founder of the United States of America by checking out: The National Endowment for the Humanities at http://edsitement.neh.gov/launchpad-benjamin-franklins-virtues.

Writing the Autobiography in his 79th year, Franklin looks back to when, at age 22, he undertook "the bold and arduous project of arriving at moral perfection." He wanted to live without committing any fault. He wanted to conquer all that natural inclination, custom and tradition, or the company of others might lead him to wrongly do. He wanted in short to reform himself, by himself, in order to possess full self-command. Alas, he discovered that this was no easy task. Bad habits and wayward inclinations continued to lead him astray. He therefore decided to undertake a more methodical approach. Directions: This Launchpad, adapted from www.WhatSoProudlyWeHail.org provides background materials and discussion questions to enhance your reading and understanding of Benjamin Franklin's "The Project of Moral Perfection" a passage from his *Autobiography*. After learning about the author, read the excerpt below along with the questions. You can click on the videos to hear editors Amy A. Kass and Leon R. Kass converse with guest host Wilfred McClay (University of Tennessee-Chattanooga) about the essay. These videos are meant to raise additional questions and enhance discussion, not replace it. This will help to see the new words in "The Portals of LIFE" in context.

The process is easy and allows the reader to use all the ways they have to learn thru my stories, thru their own writing in the journal, by watching films associated with the word, or by reading books that will enlighten and delight the reader.

Please check the appendix for a list of all the suggested books and films.

About the Author

Judi Weisbart is first and foremost a wife, mother, daughter, sister and friend because these relationships hold the essence of a successful life. She is also an author, consultant, artist, speaker and trainer. Her company *A Busy Woman* consults with non-profit organizations, individuals and businesses to create mission driven events and branding that connects the purpose to community and in their lives. She has worked as a senior consultant for the Adizes Institute and has held the position of program director and teacher for an Economic Development Corporation, Women's Economic Ventures (WEV). She has successfully created community coalitions designed to enhance financial and physical health and well being of all citizens.

Her international experience includes: featured speaker at the International Jewish Women Conference in Israel; presenting entrepreneurial training programs for women in Hungary, where she received a certificate of Honor from the Hungarian Government; and designing and implementing a corporate training program for female employees of a large corporation in Mexico. She sits on the advisory committee for Women, Culture and Development at University of California, Santa Barbara Legal Aid Foundation, Life-Chronicles, Lobero Theater, Profant Foundation for the Arts, Casa Serena and Teaching Fair.

In addition to her businesses, Judi has volunteered for a number of events. She produced International Women's Day 2003 for over 1000 people, Anne Frank in the World Exhibit in 1997, educating 10,000 local school children about the Holocaust; the Henrietta Marie Slave Ship Exhibition in 2001 with over 8,000 school children attending to learn about slavery and how they can prevent racism and hate in their communities.

Judi has moderated a number of panels, discussions and focus groups on social justice issues. Her passion is to inspire all to find their purpose in this world and play their role to make it a better place for all.

Attitude

Attitude

THE AUTHOR'S MEANING:

Attitude is the choice of how you react, respond and become pro active in your life

THE DICTIONARY DEFINITION

Attitude is a noun

- a complex mental state involving beliefs and feelings and values and dispositions to act in certain ways; he had the attitude that work was fun;

- position or arrangement of the body and its limbs; he assumed an attitude of surrender;

- a theatrical pose created for effect; the actor struck just the right attitude;

- position of aircraft or spacecraft relative to a frame of reference (the horizon or direction of motion)

> The greatest discovery of my generation is that human beings can alter their lives by altering their attitude of mind......
>
> — William James

YOUR ATTITUDE IS ONE OF THE AREAS OF YOUR LIFE THAT you can change. It is a choice how you act and respond to life. It is your attitude that defines who you are and who you want to become. It is important to understand how your attitude affects your daily inner life and how that in turn affects the world around you.

In my experience I have found that my attitude has given me insight into myself, if I am willing to look. When my husband was starting a new business I had a baby and two-step children at home it was a lot of work and I became very upset by his travel schedule. I found myself alone for weeks on end and after many months of this began to have an attitude of resentment because I felt he was hurting our family and relationship by his absence. My anger and resentment grew until one day when I changed my attitude. Instead of seeing him as an absent partner, father and husband, I imagined him as a lover. I pretended that I was a single mother with a boy-friend who was a pilot, who visited me on occasion bringing with him gifts for me and to my children. He would take me out for romantic dinners, make love to me and bring joy to my family. This silly story made me laugh and I realize that if I could change my attitude about him and the absence of his physical presence I could enjoy the time I had with him instead of resenting him for the time he was away from us. It was magic! I began a new love affair with my husband and he had a happy wife and family when he returned form those long business trips. It took only a moment to change the course of my life by changing the attitude towards the situation.

This week is the first adventure into the wisdom of self. You have an outline of steps that you can take to look at your attitude and your deep-seated beliefs. As we all know there are many ways to learn and writing is one. It will give you a window into your own soul. By answering the questions you will have a framework to begin your conversation. For others there is the joy of reading and digesting other ways to view the world, there are suggestions in this area and last but not least there is the joy of watching a great movie. The process, which you are about to embark, gives you the freedom to choose the way to look at **Attitude**.

Enjoy the journey and remember to give yourself the *light, insight, foundation* and *empowerment* you need to build a balances LIFE inside and out.

Journal:

1) This week's journal begins with a journey back into your life. Look at 5 years at a time and think about the attitudes you had at 5-10 years, 10- 15 years, 15-20 and so on.

2) If you are sad, lonely and negative most of the day ask yourself why and write those answers down. If you feel joy, happiness and fulfilled write down the reasons for your positive attitude. This is the process to understand the inner workings of you.

3) Recreate the most vivid memory of a good outcome to a bad situation and write down what you did to help make it a positive experience.

Books:

Think and Grow Rich by Napoleon Hill

Napoleon Hill was an American author who was one of the earliest producers of the modern genre of personal success literature. His most famous work, Think & Grow Rich, is one of the best selling books of his time. Hill's work examined the power of personal beliefs and the role that they play in personal success.

The Power of Positive Thinking by Norman Vincent Peale

Dr. Norman Vincent Peale was a Protestant preacher and author most notably of The Power of Positive Thinking and a progenitor of the theory of positive thinking. Peale's works came under criticism from several mental health experts; one of who directly said Peale was a con man and a fraud. These critics appeared in the early 1950s after the publication of *The Power of Positive Thinking*.

Films:

Life is Beautiful directed by Roberto Benigni starring Roberto Benigni, Nicoletta Braschi and Giorgio Cantarini.

In 1930s Italy, a carefree Jewish bookkeeper named Guido starts a fairy tale life by courting and marrying a lovely woman from a nearby city. Guido and his wife have a son and live happily together until the occupation of Italy by German forces. In an attempt to hold his family together and help his son survive the horrors of a Jewish Concentration Camp, Guido imagines that the Holocaust is a game and that the grand prize for winning is a tank.

A Beautiful Mind directed by Ron Howard starring Russell Crowe, Ed Harris & Jennifer Connelly

The Story begins in the early years of a young schizophrenic prodigy named Jonathan Nash. Early in the movie Nash begins developing paranoid schizophrenia and endures delusional episodes while painfully watching the loss and burden his condition puts on this wife and friends.

Robot and Frank directed by Jake Schreier starring Frank Langella & Susan Sarandon

The children (James Marsden and Liv Tyler) of an aging ex-convict named Frank (Frank Langella) hire a robot (voiced by Peter Sarsgaard) to care for their father. Initially wary of the robot's presence in his life, Frank warms up to his new companion and uses him to commit a heist in order to win the affection of the local librarian (Susan Sarandon).

Beauty

Beauty

THE AUTHOR'S MEANING:
Beauty is in the heart of the beholder

THE DICTIONARY DEFINITION
Beauty is a noun

- the qualities that give pleasure to the senses

- a very attractive or seductive looking woman

- an outstanding example of its kind; his roses were beauties; when I make a mistake its a beauty.

> "The best and most beautiful things in the world cannot be seen nor touched but are felt in the heart"
>
> — Helen Keller

IT IS SAID THAT BEAUTY IS IN THE EYES OF THE BEHOLDER, but I believe beauty prevails in the heart. The appreciation, existence, and recognition of beauty shapes our outlook on life and affects the way we live it. Beauty is infused in our lives by characterizing our perceptions of self and society. It is a gift to our souls, elevating us to the knowledge that LIFE is filled with experiences of the heart.

Within each of us exists the beauty of our inner child, or our true self. To see the beauty in the world around us, it is important to first find the beauty within ourselves. When I focus on the obsession of my gray hairs, weight, or wrinkles, I forget to look at the beauty in my life that exists outside myself. For instance, I become unmindful of the cornucopia of flowers filling my garden, or ignorant of the love in the eyes of my dog when I arrive home. The different expressions of what is beautiful in the world changes the way it is comprehended. Defining beauty in the Madison Ave tradition of a 19 year old, 5'11," 102 lb. model, destroys self-esteem and fosters unrealistic views of perfection in society. We struggle to fit the many, and ever changing, idealizations of beauty, at times pushing our bodies and minds to extremes. Acknowledgement and appreciation of beauty in all forms prompts the opening of our hearts to beauty in the world. We must ask ourselves why beauty is significant to society, but more importantly, how we define it ourselves.

To me beauty means many things, and its various portrayals carry significance because within beauty we can find truth and joy. For example, I have been given the gift of art in my life, and I love to create and appreciate it. Art is a gift because it is a lens allowing me to see beauty in everything around me. In art we often see colors and shapes as the basis of any work, but it is their application on a canvas that creates the dynamic for art: a space to reveal true beauty. My hope is to witness beauty in my life and experience gratitude, until one day, I look out a window and see the magnificence of beauty encompassing every moment of our lives. With gratitude, we can comprehend the attraction toward beauty, and strengthen the pleasure in our surroundings and ourselves.

Valuing the beauty in the world allows us to value the beauty in ourselves. Since beauty is molded close to our hearts, it is important that we realize the variations of beauty, as it exists around us. By doing so, we can grow toward a model of acceptance and understanding of true beauty. On this week's journey, we can learn to value our embodiment of what appeals to us, and by doing so, glorify our own beauty. We will become children living in the arms of beauty, celebrated like the colorful dance of the setting sun.

Where do you see beauty? Is it in nature, a face, or inside you?

Journal:

1) This week will bring you the joy of stopping to smell the roses... feel the beauty. Write in your journal about a beautiful memory or create one for yourself this week.

2) Go inside and talk to the inner child and ask what he/she finds to be beautiful, come at this from the eyes of a child.

3) Treat yourself to a walk on the beach, a visit to an art museum, or read a beautiful coffee table book, and then write down what you felt about the beauty you enjoyed.

Books:

Sophia Loren's Recipes and Memories by Sophia Loren

Sophia Loren is more than a beloved movie star–she's a cook. The author of two personal cookbooks, she's been recognized by the Italian government for her culinary prowess. In Sophia Loren's Recipes and Memories, she offers a hundred or so recipes arranged by course–antipasti through desserts. The recipes are models of clarity, and Sophia's introductory notes and other asides leave no doubt that the author is a serious, passionate cook. Reading her book and trying her recipes, we come to applaud the star in her apron as well as on the screen.

How, then, Shall We Live? Four Simple Questions that Reveal the Beauty and Meaning in Our Lives by Wayne Muller

Wayne Muller is an ordained minister, psychotherapist, and best-selling author. A graduate of Harvard Divinity School, he has spent the last twenty-five years working closely with some of the most disadvantaged members of society. He founded Bread for the Journey, a national, nonprofit charity serving the poor and under-privileged. Muller's mediation on four simple questions takes him far afield into revealing much of himself, the struggles and victories of the many he helps and into beautiful, illustrative literature and stories from world religions. At the end of each section he has inventive exercises that help the reader find her answer to these immortal questions.

Films:

Mask directed by Peter Bogdanovich starring Cher & Sam Elliot

Mask is a 1985 American biographical drama film directed by Peter Bogdanovich, starring Cher, Sam Elliott, and Eric Stoltz. Dennis Burkley and Laura Dern are featured in supporting roles. Cher received the 1985 Cannes Film Festival award for Best Actress. The film is based on the life and early death of Roy L. "Rocky" Dennis, a boy who suffered from craniodiaphyseal dysplasia, an extremely rare disorder known commonly as lionitis due to the disfiguring cranial enlargements that it causes. Mask won the Academy Award for Best Makeup while Cher and Stoltz received Golden Globe nominations for their performances.

On Beauty directed by Joanna Rudnick

On Beauty follows former fashion photographer Rick Guidotti, who after fifteen years of working for clients such as Yves Saint Laurent, Elle, and Harpers Bazaar, grew tired of seeing the same ideal of beauty "spit up at us constantly." Disillusioned by the industry, in a moment of serendipity, Rick walked by a young woman with

Albinism (a genetic condition that results in loss of pigmentation in the hair and eyes) at a New York city bus stop, and wondered why she wasn't considered beautiful in his other world. This exploration resulted in a show-stopping magazine spread for Life Magazine featuring young women with Albinism smiling out from under the headline "Redefining Beauty." On Beauty weaves Rick's fight to challenge public perceptions of difference with the lives of three women, who have overcome rejection by their peers, brazenly stood up to society's inability to accept difference, triumphed over their own physical obstacles.

Courage

Courage

THE AUTHOR'S MEANING:

Courage is the gift given to those who transmute their fears

THE DICTIONARY DEFINITION

Courage is a noun

- a quality of spirit that enables you to face danger of pain without showing fear.

> The ultimate measure of a man is not where he stands in moments of comfort, but where he stands at times of challenge and controversy.
>
> — Martin Luther King Jr

COURAGE EXISTS IN THE MOMENTS WHEN FEAR IS WILLINGLY transformed into a fuel propelling us toward greatness. It is evident in everyone and is one of the deepest strengths of a human being. Courage is a characteristic defining our ability to adapt to different situations by facing our fears and vulnerabilities, molding us into stronger individuals.

Reading Anne Frank's diary inspired my first courageous experience. I was fifteen years old and living in England. My father had passed away six years earlier and my mother decided to take my brother and me to her home in Northern England. I was born to a Jewish father and often felt like an outsider in the English Christian society, not realizing how different I was until the memorable day I chose to embrace my courage. While attending a party with some friends, an older boy, whom I did not know, spoke out. In a loud and drunken voice he proclaimed hate for "all yanks and yids". I was horrified and scared by his out burst and in that moment I remembered my promise to stand up against injustice and I challenged myself to face my vulnerability and take action. I would hide the Anne Frank's of the world and I would do something to act against cruelty. And so I did. I stood up to the bully, I walked up to him, slapped his face and said, "I am an American and a Jew and you are an idiot"

For the first time in my life courage emerged through my actions and all I had to do was take the risk. I was terrified at what the consequences might entail but when he backed down I was conscious of the change in myself.

Since that moment, I have marched in the streets against political inequities, stood up to a man who tried to rob me and argued for my child to be accepted into a school he wanted to attend. We need courage in all our lives, for our children, a sick loved one, or even the person standing next to us. This week challenge your understanding of courage and push yourself a step forward. Our courage blossoms through our actions and in this week's journey overcome your fears and embrace your ability to act.

Where is your courage? Have you looked for it in others?

Journal:

1) Do you remember a time you mustered up the courage to ask for a raise, confront a bigot, stood up for a child? Write the experience in your journal.

2) Who do you look up to as a courageous person in your life or in history? Explain why you see them in this light and why.

3) What does courage mean to you in today's world? Has it changed in your lifetime?

Books:

What Color is your Parachute? by Richard Nelson Bolles

For forty years now job-hunters and career-changers have been turning to this, the world's most popular job-hunting book, confident that each new annual edition will give them the most up-to-date information about the job-market and how to find meaningful work–even in the midst of challenging economic times such as these. The new ideas are wrapped around the familiar core message of Parachute: WHAT, WHERE, and HOW, with an emphasis on finding your passion and identifying your best transferable skills. With fresh insights into resumes, networking, interviewing, salary negotiation, and how to start your own business, this book will give you the tools, exercises, and motivation you need to find hope, land a job, and fulfill your purpose in life. In the words of Fortune magazine: "Parachute remains the gold standard of career guides."

The Aladdin Factor by Jack Canfield and Mark Victor Hansen

Somebody stop me! I am in the midst of further changing my life for the better and found a pot of gold at the end of the rainbow in the book The Aladdin Factor by the New York Times bestselling authors of Chicken Soup for the Soul - Jack Canfield and Mark Victor Hansen. Life is great people and we each have a specific task to fulfill during our lifetime! If you need a jump-start in awaking, finding or rededicating yourself to your purpose in life then this is the book and a great tool to utilize!

Now on to the content of the book, throughout the first two sections of the book the authors creatively include their wisdom and the lessons they wish to bestow upon the reader hidden in the story of Aladdin and the magic lamp with the genie. This approach is both entertaining and enlightening, and keeps the reader's attention focused on the overall theme of the story, but also leaves the reader subconsciously taking mental notes of the information presented for personal use once the book has been completed.

One Thousand White Women by Jim Fergus

The premise of the story is that the Northern Cheyenne Indians are shrinking in numbers and seek a way to assimilate into white society. They decide to marry white women and have half-blood children, enabling the two cultures to blend naturally. The Cheyenne Chief Little Wolf approaches President Ulysses Grant with the proposal to trade 1000 white women for 1000 horses, an offer publicly refused by the government. However, the government sees the placating of the Indians as being to their benefit, so they begin the "Brides for Indians" program in which women who are physically healthy and of child rearing age may volunteer to go. However, in order to keep the plan unpublished, they offer the trip to women in prison, asylums, and other restrictive situations.

Films:

Julia directed by Fred Zimmerman with Jane Fonda and Vanessa Redgrave

Julia is a 1977 film made by 20th Century Fox. It is based on Lillian Hellman's book Pentimento, a chapter of which purports to tell the story of her relationship with an alleged lifelong friend, "Julia," who fought against the Nazis in the years prior to World War II.

The young Lillian and the young Julia, daughter of a wealthy family being brought up by her grandparents in the U.S., enjoy a childhood together and an extremely close relationship in late adolescence. Later, while medical-student/physician Julia (Vanessa Redgrave) attends Oxford and the University of Vienna and studies with such luminaries as Sigmund Freud, Lillian (Jane Fonda) suffers through revisions of her play with her mentor and sometime lover, famed author Dashiell Hammett (Jason Robards) at a beach house.

Milk directed by Gus Van Sant with Sean Penn & Josh Brolin

This is a 2008 Academy Award winner Sean Penn takes the title role in Gus Van Sant's biopic tracing the last eight years in the life of Harvey Milk, the ill-fated politician and gay activist whose life changed history, and whose courage still inspires people. When Milk was elected to the San Francisco Board of Supervisors in 1977, he made history for being the first openly gay man in American history to be voted into public office. But the rights of homosexuals weren't Milk's primary concern, as tellingly evidenced by the wide array of political coalitions he formed over the course of his tragically brief career. He fought for everyone from union workers to senior citizens, a true hero of human rights who possessed nothing but compassion for his fellow man. The story begins in New York City, where a 40-year-old Milk ponders what steps he can take to make his life more meaningful. ~ Jason Buchanan

Man of La Mancha directed by Arthur Heller with Sophia Loren & Peter O'Toole

This is a 1972 film adaptation of the Broadway musical *Man of La Mancha* by Dale Wasserman, with music by Mitch Leigh and lyrics by Joe Darion. The musical was suggested by the classic novel *Don Quixote de la Mancha* by Miguel de Cervantes, but more directly based on Wasserman's 1959 non-musical television play, *I, Don Quixote,* which combines a semi-fictional episode from the life of Cervantes with scenes from his novel. The Spanish Inquisition has imprisoned Cervantes and his manservant, and a manuscript by Cervantes is seized by his fellow inmates, who subject him to a mock trial in order to determine whether the manuscript should be returned. Cervantes' defense is in the form of a play, in which Cervantes takes the role of Alonso Quijano, an old gentleman who has lost his mind and now believes that he should go forth as a knight-errant. Quijano renames himself Don Quixote de La Mancha, and sets out to find adventures with his "squire", Sancho Panza.

Discipline

Discipline

THE AUTHOR'S MEANING:

Discipline is the underpinning to the structure of success

THE DICTIONARY DEFINITION

Discipline is both a noun and a verb

- a branch of knowledge; in what discipline is his doctorate? teachers should be well trained in their subject; anthropology is the study of human beings; Parents must discipline their children; Is this dog trained?;

- a system of rules of conduct or method of practice; he quickly learned the discipline of prison routine; for such a plan to work requires discipline;

- the trait of being well behaved; he insisted on discipline among the troops;

- training to improve strength or self-control

- the act of punishing; the offenders deserved the harsh discipline they received;

- verb

- train by instruction and practice; especially to teach self-control;

- punish in order to gain control or enforce obedience; The teacher disciplined the pupils rather frequently;

> Great works are performed not
> by strength but by perseverance ...
>
> — Samuel Johnson

DISCIPLINE IS A VIRTUE MANY OF US FIND DIFFICULT TO foster. A life without discipline can be distressing, as it is the underpinning of all success. Discipline gives us a better sense of self and gives insight to our abilities. For men, discipline is viewed in a physical manner. They are more inclined to believe in the Marine image of discipline, testing their control through their bodies: "100 push-ups now!" For women, discipline is more concerned with the mind, pushing their mental and emotional constraints. Although the mental and physical mediums of discipline may be more evident in one sex than the other, they are not gender specific.

When we see discipline as a negative we shy away from it, and fail to take advantage of its benefits. The conscious effort toward self-discipline will help encourage your growth. For example, I have learned to discipline myself through a consistent swimming regimen: five times a week for twenty minutes a day. My life has changed as a result of my ability to discipline myself for this exercise. I've grown to be more productive, feel stronger, and enjoy more stamina in all I do. This was only accomplished with the help of my husband's eight-year campaign, motivating me to work out. He was right, and because I can see the results, I have formed a new discipline for my body and myself.

The need for discipline is imperative in a child's life. It is not spanking or yelling, taking away privileges or time-outs, but more specifically, it is consistent consequences to certain behaviors. These responses will gradually enlighten children of proper demeanor and encourage their growth in a learning environment as they prepare for 'the real world.' All parents understand the difficulty in consistent discipline of a child, especially as they enter their teens. The following memory might help us all alleviate concern around this subject. When my stepson was twelve years old, my husband and I were in a harrowing court battle for custody of him and his sisters. I asked him why he wanted to live with us instead of his mother, and his response floored me: "I want to live with you and dad because in this house I learn discipline and if I don't learn it now, how will I have self discipline when I am an adult?" Wow, did that say it all! I was shocked at his level of insight, and realized children need to be taught through loving consistent actions. Discipline is important to our growth and survival as self-sufficient adults, and with the right support, it will allow us to proposer.

Your willingness to devote one week to this chapter is a discipline in itself. It demands focus, determination, time management, and organization. Through these components, you can establish a discipline in yourself that will help you finish what you start, overcome your discomforts, and ultimately feel fulfillment and self esteem.

Do you have a discipline in your life, a daily routine and structure?

Journal:

1) Look at yourself and see where discipline will help you to grow. For me the discipline of writing this book has been a struggle but a reward beyond my wildest dreams. What do you need to do for yourself?

2) Is there a place in your life where you have created a strong self-discipline?

3) Do you remember who taught you to be disciplined, if anyone? If you cannot think of a teacher then think of what experience you have had with discipline. For many of us it is negative. Write down your feelings and memories, this might be the insight that you need to change your life for the better and work towards those things you thought impossible.

Books:

The Fifth Discipline: The Art and Practice of the Learning Organization

A book by Peter Senge (a senior lecturer at MIT) focusing on group problem solving using the systems thinking method in order to convert companies into learning organizations. The five disciplines represent approaches (theories and methods) for developing three core-learning capabilities: fostering aspiration, developing reflective conversation, and understanding complexity.

Celebrating discipline: the path to spiritual growth by Richard J. Foster

In the twenty years since its publication, Celebration of Discipline has helped over a million seekers discover a richer spiritual life infused with joy, peace, and a deeper understanding of God. For this special twentieth anniversary edition, Richard J. Foster has added an introduction, in which he shares the story of how this beloved and enduring spiritual guidebook came to be. Hailed by many as the best modern book on Christian spirituality, Celebration of Discipline explores the "classic Disciplines," or central spiritual practices, of the Christian faith. Along the way, Foster shows that it is only by and through these practices that the true path to spiritual growth can be found. Dividing the Disciplines into three movements of the Spirit, Foster shows how each of these areas contribute to a balanced spiritual life. The inward Disciplines of meditation, prayer, fasting, and study, offer avenues of personal examination and change.

Films:

Apollo 13 directed by Ron Howard with Tom Hanks, Bill Paxton & Kevin Bacon

A movie based on what was to be the third lunar-landing mission. This film shows the trials and tribulations of the Apollo 13 crew, mission control, and families after a near-fatal accident cripples the space vehicle. A mission that couldn't get TV airtime because space flights had become routine to the American public suddenly grabbed the national spotlight. This is a tale of averted tragedy, heroism and shows a testament to the creativity of the scientists who ran the early space missions.

Karate Kid Director: John G. Avildsen with Ralph Macchio, Pat Morita and Elisabeth Shue

Daniel LaRusso is new in town, and is getting picked on by the local bullies, who are adept in karate. Determined to stick up for himself, Daniel begins to teach himself karate, only to discover that the caretaker at his apartment seems to be a grand master in karate. Agreeing to teach Daniel, Mr. Miyagi shows Daniel that there is more to karate than violence, and perhaps the best way to solve the problem he has with the bullies is in the All Valley Karate Championship.

Harts War directed by Gregory Hoblit with Bruce Willis, Colin Farrel & Terrence Howard

Belgium, December 16, 1944: First Lieutenant Thomas Hart (Farrell) is captured by German commandos during the opening of the Battle of the Bulge. Taken to a local prison, his boots are confiscated and he is left naked in a cell. Threatened with frostbite and pneumonia, he is coerced into divulging intelligence to his German interrogator. After a trial to determine who killed Bedford, the German camp commandant, Visser orders everyone out and announces that Hart will be shot there and then. After the head count is short by 35 prisoners, Visser suspects an escape plot and locates the tunnel. Now fully aware of the deception, he furiously orders everybody at the trial to be shot as well. But before the sentence is carried out, McNamara, moved by Hart's selfless sacrifice, voluntarily returns to the camp to accept responsibility. At that moment the factory blows up and the other escapees scatter away.

Visser holds McNamara accountable and personally executes him on the spot, sparing the remaining prisoners. Hart leads the salute to McNamara's dead body. Three months later, the German army surrenders to the Allies and the prison camp is liberated.

Environment

Environment

THE AUTHOR'S MEANING:

Environment is the surrounding that sustains the mind, body and spirit

THE DICTIONARY DEFINITION

Environment is a noun

- the totality of surrounding conditions; he longed for the comfortable environment of his livingroom;

- the area in which something exists or lives; the country- the flat agricultural surround;

> Our environment, the world in which we live and work, is a mirror of our attitudes and expectations.
>
> — Earl Nightingale

BEING CONSCIOUS OF OUR SURROUNDING ENVIRONMENT IS important on many levels because it affects how we function and compose our physical and mental conditions. The physical environment we live in affects our body through our health, and can either strengthen or weaken us. Likewise, our emotional environment can strain our mental state and injure our personal lives. Such constraints on the body and mind can challenge our perceptions, and strain our capabilities.

It begins as a matter of survival. As a nation, the environment depicts security and health, and as individuals, it shapes our serenity and emotional balance. These domains are composed by what we see, what we feel, and what we do. On the global level, I believe destroying the environment we live in destroys our homes, our community and our future. The steps we take to provide a clean and stable home for our families is the manner in which we need to treat our communities. The lack of concern for our future will result in a planetary disaster, impairing the way we live. We lose species on the earth frequently, and the negative effects of our actions must end before it threatens the human race. Our actions are influenced by our beliefs, and it is important to compose ourselves with values that will better our surroundings. By doing so, we can create emotionally healthy and stable environments in our personal lives. Decisions fueled by greed will ensure our extinction. It causes us to disregard others and pushes us into selfishness. Instead, we should focus on the values that improve our personal environments and on operations that will better our communities.

What are you doing or saying to make sure this world is a better place? Al Gore's film Inconvenient Truth proclaims it is possible to make a difference by stopping the way we harm our environment, thus changing the course of our planet's survival. The question is how to accomplish this. Nationally, we must work to lessen our pollutants from factories, cars, and all that pollute and heat up this beautiful planet.

We must demand the world governments to change their policies and views of economics. Using green products and ideas can create large new sectors for jobs and affordable products. This is important to us globally, nationally, and personally. In our homes we can create environments where we can live in balance without the clutter and chaos. This will help us in our daily lives to enjoy more, have the strength to grow and a place of solace at the end of the day. It is true that when we begin at home and in ourselves, we can change the world. Recycling, using non-chemical cleaning products, and using less electricity in our homes can be the beginning of a global shift. Our environments, from individual places of calm to global biospheres of life, all depend on our choices today. This week, consider the ways you have harmed the environments around you, and discover ways to allow your body and mind to prosper.

Have you worked on the environment? Globally, nationally or personally?

Journal:

1) This week think of issues like recycling. Do you spray pesticides instead of an old fashioned weeding? Write down your contribution to the world. Think of how you can give the next generation a home planet where they can live.

2) Work closer to home, how does your home look. Change it if it is not appealing. Look at ways to clean it up and make it a sacred place for your soul, mind and body to be at peace.

3) In what ways can you learn more about the environment? Are you involved in an organization that helps the planet? Think about what you want to do and write it in your journal.

Books:

Bounded people, Boundless Land by Eric T. Freyfogel

What right do humans have to claim sovereignty over the land, to build fences and set boundaries when nature itself recognizes no such boundaries? Is there hope for a new land ethic that is less destructive toward the land that views nature as something to be valued and nurtured rather than exploited and "developed"? One of the main challenges of contemporary environmentalism is to find a lasting, more ethical way for people to live on the planet. In Bounded People, Boundless Lands, legal scholar Eric T. Frey-fogle asks a series of pointed and challenging questions about the human quest for ecological harmony. Deftly interweaving moral and ethical considerations with case studies and real-life situations, Freyfogle provides a deep philosophical examination of personal responsibility and the dominion of human beings over the earth. He raises provocative questions about private property rights, responsible land ownership, the rights of wildlife, and ecological health.

The western guide to Feng Shui by Terah Kathryn Collins

Feng Shui teacher Terah Kathryn explains why the arrangement of readers' homes and workplaces affects every aspect of their lives, including relationships, health, and finances. This informative text takes readers on a step-by-step journey through their home and office, opening their Feng Shui eyes to see the problems and the solutions in their environment.

Films:

Baraka by Ron Fricke

A movie with no conventional plot: merely a collection of expertly photographed scenes. Subject matter has a highly environmental theme. The title *Baraka* means blessing in a multitude of languages, deriving originally from the Arabic بركة The film is often compared to *Koyaanisqatsi*, the first of the Qatsi films by Godfrey Reggio for which Fricke was cinematographer. *Baraka* was the first in over twenty years to be photographed in the 70mm Todd-AO format.

Taken for a Ride directed by Martha Olson and Jim Klein

The 55-minute film was first broadcast on August 6, 1996 on the PBS television series *POV.* Why Does America Have the Worst Public Transit in the Industrialized World, and the Most Free-ways? Taken for a Ride reveals the tragic and little known story of an auto and oil industry campaign, led by General Motors, to buy and dismantle streetcar lines. Across the nation, tracks were torn up, sometimes overnight, and diesel buses placed on city streets. The highway lobby then pushed through Congress a vast network of urban freeways that doubled the cost of the Interstates, fueled suburban development, increased auto dependence, and elicited pas-sionate opposition. Citizens who would become the leading edge of a new environmental movement stopped seventeen city freeways. With investigative journalism, vintage archival footage and candid interviews, Taken for a Ride presents a revealing history of our cities in the 20th century that is also a meditation on corporate power, city form, citizen protest and the social and environmental implications of transportation. Taken for a Ride was funded by the Independent Television Service.

Fuel directed by Josh Tickell.

It won the audience award at the 2008 Sundance Film Festival. The DVD was released on June 22, 2010. This film rocks. Every school needs FUEL shown in it. FUEL can empower the people to lead the politicians. No wonder it's getting standing ovations everywhere it has screened. No wonder it's had a Hollywood Premiere (green carpet) and begins theatrical release this month. Don't miss FUEL! In this feature-length documentary, filmmaker and biofuel advocate Josh Tickell explores the origins of America's dependence on fossil fuels, eventually detailing the cross-country road trip that he took in his biodiesel-converted van, campaigning for the more sustainable, environmentally friendly fuel. Tickell interviews people in his film from all over the spectrum of fuel use, from oil company executives to those devastated by water contamination stemming from oil companies to Midwestern families considering buying Hummers. Hoping to paint as complete a picture as possible of American fuel use, Tickell explores how we fuel our lifestyle in the present and how we can hope to in the future.

Focus

Focus

THE AUTHOR'S MEANING
Focus is a single-minded laser creating a clear consciousness

THE DICTIONARY DEFINITION
Focus is both a noun and a verb

- the concentration of attention or energy on something; the focus of activity shifted to molecular biology; he had no direction in his life; in focus; out of focus;

- maximum clarity or distinctness of an image rendered by an optical system;

- maximum clarity or distinctness of an idea; the controversy brought clearly into focus an important difference of opinion;

- a central point or locus of an infection in an organism; the focus of infection;

- special emphasis attached to something; the stress was more on accuracy than on speed;

- a point of convergence of light (or other radiation) or a point from which it diverges

- a fixed reference point on the concave side of a conic section verb

- direct one's attention on something; Please focus on your studies and not on your hobbies;

- cause to converge on or toward a central point; Focus the light on this image;

- bring into focus or alignment; to converge or cause to converge; of ideas or emotions

- become focused or come into focus; The light focused;

- put (an image) into focus;

> Our true home is in the present moment. To live in the present moment is a miracle.
>
> — Thich Nhat Han

IN MY LIFE I HAVE FOUND THAT FOCUS IS THE MOST DIFFICULT discipline. When we learn new things, make discoveries, or embark on exciting adventures, our thoughts scatter to absorb our surroundings. It is hard to foster control on the turns our mind takes from one thought to another. When creating new and exciting works my mind constantly wanders, and I have to ask myself what is important, what I want, and where my focus is. The bane of my existence is not my lack of passion, but my inability to focus. In such circumstances it is beneficial to have a form of direction and guidance to motivate attention and boost concentration. My husband is my compass, redirecting my energy with his quiet reminders to focus. Do you have a "compass," a person who keeps your mind on the task at hand? Think of the focus you need to complete your purpose. Much has been written about the discipline of meditation and its power to train the mind and body to relax. I have found this to be a very helpful. It is the place where I can go to erase the frenetic babbling of my mind and develop the focus I need to stay on track. This meditation is an excellent exercise to clear the scattered thoughts in our minds and centralize our attention.

Focus is important because it allows us to efficiently execute our tasks. By doing so, we are capable of putting in our total effort and care to the projects we undertake. The endeavors that demand our focus are the experiences that affect us the most, and reveal the greatest about our personas. The ability to exercise different levels of focus expands one's self control and determination, encouraging us forward toward our goals. Such measures allow us to experiment with our dedication, work ethic, and restraints.

One of the clearest forms of focus I have ever experienced was looking at a 3-D picture. When looked at in the correct way, or past the first level of viewing for most people, you can find focus in the photograph. It is an exciting moment when your focus is clear. In life we have this experience daily in hundreds of ways. My best example of focus is through this book. I never really focused on the work for this book when I began its composition, only devoting my attention to it for a day or two. Twelve years later, however, I am finally focusing on its completion. I work daily for one hour, have two amazing young women from UCSB as my interns working on it with me, and I am finally making a step toward its completion! This project demands a great amount of focus and concentration from all its participants, including its readers. If you have worked on the skill of focus in life, you can often see opportunities others miss as they blithely wonder without focus. This week, work on championing your focus by concentrating on the tasks you endeavor in.

What do you do to create a space where you use the skills to focus?

Journal:

1) Think of the ways you have created focus in your life.

2) Go back to a time you remember the feeling of being single minded and recreate it in the work you do this week.

3) Create a list of the areas in your life you would like to have more focus and ask yourself what steps do you need to take to accomplish this goal.

Books:

The Power of Focus Jack Canfield, MV Hansen & Les Hewitt

The No 1 reason that stops people from getting what they want is lack of focus. People, who focus on what they want, prosper. Those who don't, struggle. In The Power of Focus you'll discover the specific focusing strategies used by the world's most successful men and women. Find out how to: -Focus on your strengths and eliminate everything that is holding you back. -Change bad habits into habits that will make you debt-free and wealthy. -Create an excellent balance between work and family life - without guilt! Your ability to focus will determine your future - start now!

Manifest Your Destiny by Wayne Dyer

From the inspirational leader and author of the international best-sellers Your Sacred Self and the classic Your Erroneous Zones comes this mind-awakening guidebook for making your desires reality. Based on ancient principles and spiritual practices, Manifest Your Destiny introduces the Nine Spiritual Principles that will help you overcome the barriers–both within and around you–that prevent you from getting what you want, including: Developing spiritual awareness, Trusting yourself, Reconnecting to your environment, Accepting your own worthiness, Practicing unconditional love, Meditating to unlock the power within you, Letting go of demands, Filled with warmth and insight, this invaluable book will help you achieve your goals–and take you to a level higher than you've ever dreamed.

Films:

Million Dollar Baby directed by Clint Eastwood with Hilary Swank & Morgan Freeman

A hardened trainer/manager works with a determined woman in her attempt to establish herself as a boxer. *Million Dollar Baby* is a 2004 sports drama film directed, co-produced, and scored by Clint Eastwood and starring Eastwood, Hilary Swank, and Morgan Freeman. It is the story of an under-appreciated boxing trainer, his elusive past, and his quest for atonement by helping an under-dog amateur boxer, the film's title character, achieves her dream of becoming a professional. The film won four Academy Awards, including Best Picture.

Hugo directed by Martin Scorsese

This is a 2011 American 3D adventure drama film based on Brian Selznick's novel *The Invention of Hugo Cabret* about a boy who lives alone in a Paris railway station. It is directed and co-produced by Martin Scorsese and adapted for the screen by John Logan. Hugo lives between the walls of the station, maintaining the clocks, stealing food and working on his father's most ambitious project: repairing a broken automaton, a mechanical man who is supposed to write with a pen. Convinced the automaton contains a message from his father, Hugo goes to desperate lengths to fix it. He steals mechanical parts to repair the automaton, but he is caught by a toy storeowner, Papa Georges (Ben Kingsley), who takes Hugo's notebook from him, with notes and drawings for fixing the automaton.

Giving

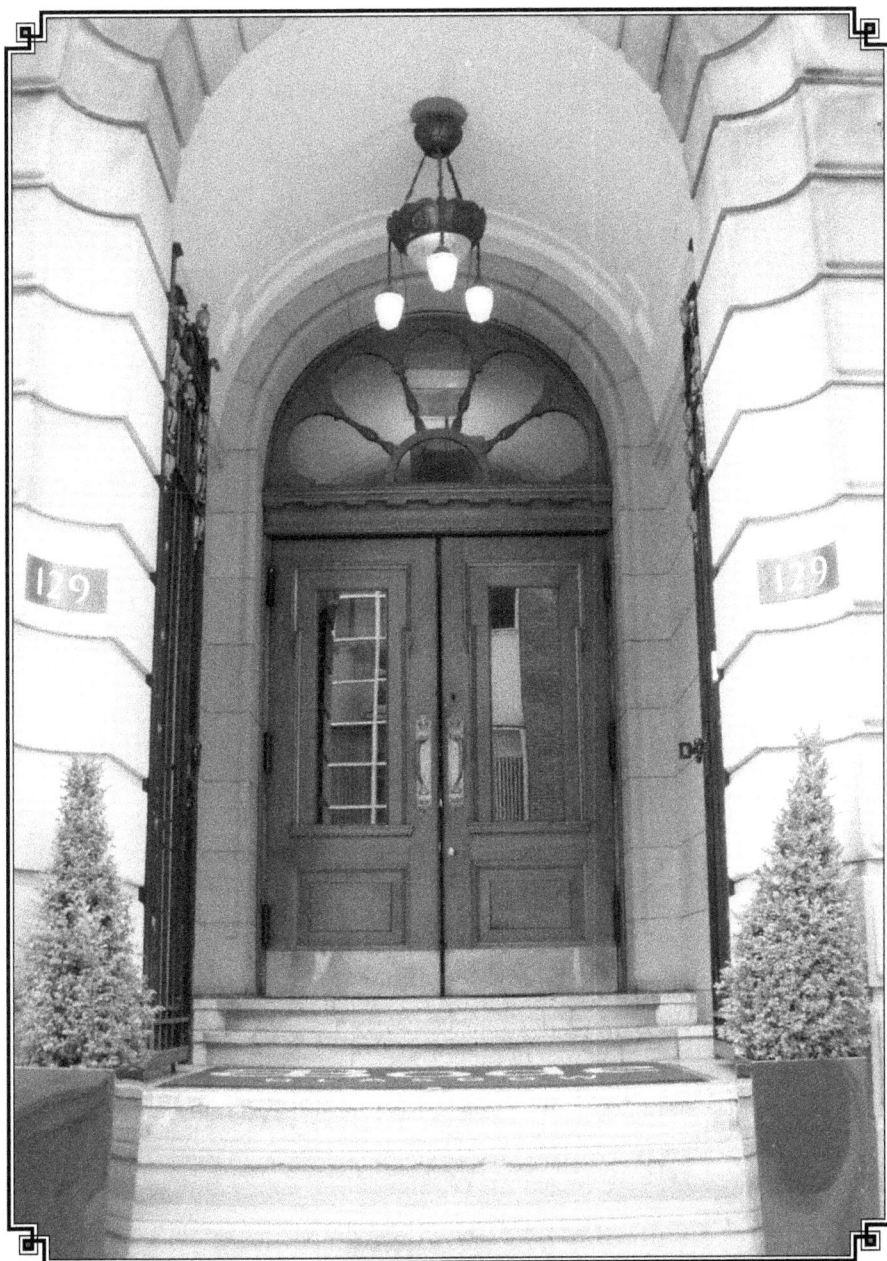

Giving

THE AUTHOR'S MEANING
Giving is the light given to us by the receiver

THE DICTIONARY DEFINITION
Giving is an adjective and noun

- given or giving freely; was a big tipper; the bounteous goodness of God; bountiful compliments; a freehanded host; a handsome allowance; Saturday's child is loving and giving; a liberal backer of the arts; a munificent gift; her fond and openhanded grandfather; the alumni followed a program of annual giving; noun

- the act of giving

- the imparting of news or promises etc.; he gave us the news and made a great show of the giving; giving his word of honor seemed to come too easily;

- disposing of property by voluntary transfer without receiving value in return;

> Complete possession is proved only by giving. All you are unable to give possesses you.
>
> — Andre Gide

GIVING EXISTS AS ITS OWN CYCLE IN NATURE. IT IS AN ACT OF selflessness for the betterment of another group or individual. Like opening and closing, up and down, or life and death, giving is the counterpart to the act of receiving. Giving must be viewed as one half of the whole–as one gives, the other receives.

The gratitude one has in receiving should be reflected in the act of giving. Understanding how to give to another person in such a manner is the direct result of receiving something from another individual in the same condition. For example, if someone gives you a gift as an appreciation for a kind act you did, you are likely to convey the same attitude to him or her when the exchange is reversed and they receive a gift from you. We are more likely to react a certain way as a reflection of the behavior that is around us. Therefore, if we have received a gift in a kind and loving manner, it is highly probable for us to reflect the same emotions.

The gifts of love, money or objects, can only be given if the giver first received them. Giving unconditionally to a beggar, child, or a family member can be rewarding in ways that are unimaginable. My mother always said, "It is better to give than to receive." I think she is right because by giving you feel like a good person, and that power soothes your ego. That is why the receiving must be worked on in coordination with the giving, since the act of receiving can be difficult, and often least valued part of the exchange. To receive is a blessing, but at times it can be an embarrassment and must be learned for the energy of the exchange to gratify both parties. I learned it the hard way, but I will be forever grateful that I did.

In my late twenties, as a young mother and passionate young woman, a dreadful and potentially fatal disease that changed my life forever struck me. I could not get out of bed without severe pain, I was unable to carry my three-year-old child, make love to my husband, or shop on my own. I became depressed and felt useless. My mother and husband looked at me with sad and sympathetic eyes. They brought me food, cared for my needs, and were my strength and lifeline. I needed them, but I often felt uncomfortable and angry when they did so much for me. It took me a long time to see the light in this exchange. I realized that if I accepted their gifts they would feel that they were of use and were making my life a little better. When they felt those emotions they were less saddened by my condition, and it elevated their energy because it elevated mine. The ability of receiving with love, joy and gratitude makes the giving that much sweeter.

This week allocate some of your time to the practice of giving. Consider the way you give to others, and the manner in which you receive from them. Our actions are the reflections of others, and influence the how others act as well. Strive to give in a positive light, and make your exchanges in life beneficial to all ends. Giving is an art and a blessing. This week be aware of the gifts you are given and how you receive them.

Journal:

1. Make a list of the gifts you give this week. Remember gifts are more than financial and literal. They do not have to be things they can be actions such as the ones my family gave me during my illness.

2. How do you see giving in your life? Do you come from a family that always gave presents instead of love? Does your family and friends consist of giving people or are they takers? Think back to times when you felt unconditional love from another and when you gave it.

3. What is your perspective on your giving and receiving? Do you do both with joy and gratitude? Do you do one more than the other? If so why? Can you see your patterns and do you want to change them?

Books:

'The Giving Tree' by Shel Silverberg

The Giving Tree is a tale about a relationship between a young boy and a tree. The tree always provides the boy with what he wants: branches on which to swing, shade in which to sit and apples to eat. As the boy grows older, he requires more and more of the tree. The tree loves the boy very much and gives him anything he asks for. In an ultimate act of self-sacrifice, the tree lets the boy cut it down so the boy can build a boat in which he can sail. The boy leaves the tree, now a stump. Many years later, the boy, now an old man, returns, and the tree sadly says: "I'm sorry, boy... but I have nothing left to give you." But the boy replies: "I do not need much now, just a quiet place to sit and rest." The tree then says, "Well, an old tree stump is a good place for sitting and resting. Come, boy, sit down and rest." The boy obliges and the tree is very happy.

The Power of Giving - Authors Harvey McKinnon & Azim Jamal

The Power of Giving is a book about you and your potential. It's really a book about how each of us lives our life, and how you can improve yours. The surprise is that you can improve every part of your own life by giving.

Films:

Aemelie: Amélie Poulain

Audrey Tautou is a young woman who had grown up isolated from other children. After the death of her mother and her father's subsequent withdrawal, she developed an unusually active imagination to ward away the feelings of loneliness. Amelie is the story of a shy waitress, played by Audrey Tautou, who decides to change the lives of those around her for the better, while struggling with her own isolation. Amelie's good deeds are eventually reciprocated by karma as she meets a young man named Nino Quincampoix who is equally as quirky as her.

The Soloist: directed by Joe Wright starring Jamie Foxx and Robert Downey Jr.

The film is based on a true story of Nathaniel Ayers, a musician who develops schizophrenia and becomes homeless. Foxx portrays Ayers, who is considered a cello prodigy, and Downey portrays Lopez, a *Los Angeles Times* columnist who discovers Ayers and writes about him in the newspaper. While speaking with Mary, his ex-wife, Lopez realizes that not only has he changed Ayers' life, Ayers has changed him. Later, while all watch an orchestra, Lopez ponders how beneficial their friendship has been. Ayers still hears voices, but at least he no longer lives on the streets. In addition, Ayers has helped Lopez's relationship with his own family.

Health

Health

Health is the state of being that affects all other states

Health is a noun

- a healthy state of wellbeing free from disease; physicians should be held responsible for the health of their patients;

- the general condition of body and mind; his delicate health; in poor health

> Health is the greatest gift, contentment the greatest wealth, faithfulness the best relationship.
>
> — Buddha

LIFE IS A GIFT BUT WITHOUT HEALTH IT CAN BE A BURDEN. Health is one state of being we all need to be happy and productive individuals. I have been unhealthy many times in my life, and I must admit it was very difficult. The saying, "I have been poor and rich and the latter is preferable," is also true for "illness and health," the latter *is* preferable! Though being healthy is an optimum state, illness is a condition that can endow many of us with great lessons through the experience. Being ill was a circumstance where I became more knowledgeable about acceptance, compassion, patience, and humility, though I am not suggesting that illness is the best way to learn these virtues. An illness, such as the common cold or pneumonia, can leave us in a vulnerable circumstance; our dependency on care can enlighten us. Instead, I suggest that health should be premier in your life to experience life lessons and virtues in a positive manner. Health is a place one can do great things. Keep it, work at it, and enjoy it.

When our bodies are healthy our minds are healthy. Eating right, exercising, and obtaining plenty of rest are a few steps to a healthier lifestyle. Changing our diet by straying away from unhealthy foods, such as sweets and fast food meals, can improve our mood, brighten our skin, and leave us feeling better about ourselves. Exercise allows us to put both our bodies and minds in better shape. Burning calories can leave us feeling in control and improve our image, but most importantly, it keeps our bodies fit and in shape. Pushing our bodies physically is as important as letting ourselves get the proper amount of daily rest. Getting an extra hour of sleep can have you waking up more refreshed and in a better state of mind. We must be aware of our body and its level of ease to accomplish its highest potential. By so doing we establish a thriving vigor that can allow us to strive and better our lives.

Part of the importance of a healthy lifestyle is to prevent diseases. The word disease is often explained by those who are in the healing arts as **dis –ease,** meaning the body is no longer at ease. By maintaining a nutritional diet, regular exercise, and giving our bodies physical relief, we can better our physical conditions. Although taking these steps forward to introduce betterment to our lives, it is equally significant to remove the harmful consumptions. Putting toxins in our body, such as drugs and alcohol, can damage our system and leave deep scars in our lives emotionally and physically. Even the smallest inhale of a cigarette can inhibit one's well being. Stay focused on the betterment of your body. Feeling the difference of a healthy lifestyle can push for better stamina, state of mind, and self esteem. The better our body feels, the better we feel.

Taking the step toward a healthy lifestyle comes from within us. Although I do not have great wisdoms on this subject, I do have a few questions that may give you the drive you need this week. These questions can help you reevaluate what being healthy means, and push you to accept your responsibility of finding the way to your optimum health and joy. This week, take a chance on yourself to make a better, healthier, change in your life.

Health is a must if we are to achieve our fullest potential.

Journal:

1) This week focus on your health. Do you exercise regularly? What do you eat? Do you get enough rest? Is there someone you hug every day? All these things matter. Look at your life. Do you intentionally help your mind and body to stay healthy? If not reconsider your choices so that you can enjoy the gift of life.

2) Have you been for a physical examination by your doctor this year or seen the dentist for a cleaning? If you are a woman have you had a mammogram? Make the appointment if you have not put these things first in your mind. You must take responsibility for the upkeep of your physical vehicle - your body!

3) Spend this week writing down everything you eat and drink, and I mean everything, the cup of coffee, the potato chips, the apple, every thing. Also write down every time you exercise, the walk from the bus, the time at the gym or even the stairs you climbed. Try to write how much you did so that you can become more aware of your body. For those of you who have been on a diet and exercise plan this will be old hat, but for those of you who have never had a food and exercise journal you will be very surprised at the results.

Books:

Deepak Chopra, M.D is the author of more than 65 books, (choose one or two) including numerous *New York Times* bestsellers. His medical training is in internal medicine and endocrinology, and he is a Fellow of the American College of Physicians, a member of the American Association of Clinical Endocrinologists, and an adjunct professor of Executive Programs at the Kellogg School of Management at Northwestern University. He is also a Distinguished Executive Scholar at Columbia Business School, Columbia University, and a Senior Scientist at the Gallup organization. For more than a decade, he has participated as a lecturer at the Update in Internal Medicine, an annual event sponsored by Harvard Medical School's Department of Continuing Education and the Department of Medicine, Beth Israel Deaconess Medical Center.

You Being Beautiful by Drs. Oz and Roizen.

They break wide open the stereotypes about how we define beauty. The doctors take an informative, scientific, and entertaining approach that's designed to not only help you look younger and more beautiful but also help you truly feel younger and more beautiful. It's a total mind-body makeover that melts your belly fat, slashes your stress, rejuvenates your skin, and boosts your confidence — so you're able to live the life you want to live.

Anatomy of an Illness by Norman Cousins

This was the first book by a patient that spoke to our current interest in taking charge of our own health. It started the revolution in patients working with their doctors and using humor to boost their bodies' capacity for healing. When Norman Cousins was diagnosed with a crippling and irreversible disease, he forged an unusual collaboration with his physician, and together they were able to beat the odds. The doctor's genius was in helping his patient to use his own powers: laughter, courage, and tenacity. The patient's talent was in mobilizing his body's own natural resources, proving what an effective healing tool the mind can be. This remarkable story of the triumph of the human spirit is truly inspirational reading.

Films:

50/50 directed by Jonathan Levine

Adam discovers he has a rare cancer in his spine and must undergo chemotherapy. He sees on the Internet that his chances of survival are 50/50. Kyle attempts to keep Adam's spirits high, which include helping Adam shave his head prior to chemotherapy and suggesting that Adam use his illness as a way to pick up women. During chemo treatments, Adam also befriends Alan (Philip Baker Hall) and Mitch (Matt Frewer), two older cancer patients who are also undergoing chemotherapy.

After Mitch suddenly dies, Adam's fears become more evident upon hearing that his treatment is not working and that he needs to undertake a risky surgery as a last resort. After waiting six hours, Kyle, Diane, and Katherine are told by the doctor that although the bone degradation was worse than they had thought, the tumor was successfully removed and Adam should recover. The movie ends with Adam getting ready for a date, with Kyle encouraging him and cleaning the incision on Adam's back from the surgery.

Supersize Me directed by Morgan Spurlock

A 2004 American documentary film directed by and starring Morgan Spurlock, an American independent filmmaker. Spurlock's film follows a 30-day period from February 1 to March 2, 2003 during which he ate only McDonald's food. The film documents this lifestyle's drastic effect on Spurlock's physical and psychological well being, and explores the fast food industry's corporate influence, including how it encourages poor nutrition for its own profit.

Intimacy

Intimacy

Intimacy is the joy of knowing your authentic self and sharing it with another

THE DICTIONARY DEFINITION
Intimacy is a noun

- the state of being intimate.

- a close, familiar, and usually affectionate or loving personal relationship with another person or group.

- a close association with or detailed knowledge or deep understanding of a place, subject, period of history, etc.: an intimacy with Japan.

- an act or expression serving as a token of familiarity, affection, or the like: to allow the intimacy of using first names.

- an amorously familiar act; liberty.

But that intimacy of mutual embarrassment, in which each feels that the other is feeling something, having once existed, its effect is not to be done away with.

— George Eliot

THE WORD INTIMACY EVOKES THE IMAGE OF A COUPLE looking deep into one another's eyes at the depths of their souls, connecting on a level only few can appreciate. Through books, films, movies, and other forms of media, we are exposed to many interpretations and displays of intimacy and affection. Yes, this is one way to see intimacy, but I believe it is much more than the emotional or physical. Intimacy is not solely reserved for those in love, and it is not limited to individuals in a partnership or sexual relationship. Intimacy is a gift to those willing to open their hearts and souls to their authentic self, and share it with another person who is also willing to do the same. Being intimate relies on the ability to trust unconditionally, as it requires one to bare their innermost desires, secrets, and wishes.

This is a very frightening notion for many as it leaves us open to pain, disappointment, and rejection. When we are intimate with another person, we expose not only our souls, but our minds and hearts as well. We are left in a comprising position due to the vulnerability of revealing who we are. The act of intimacy removes society's masks and breaks the separation between individuals. In those single moments we chose to be intimate, we abandon our independence to connect two souls. To be intimate, to be true to yourself, is a challenge met by the brave souls who know in their hearts that true joy can be felt only when intimacy is present.

In my life I have been blessed with many intimate moments and relationships because I chose to surround myself with those experiences. One that comes to mind is of the day my son's girlfriend came to me and asked me to speak with her in private, away from the others in the living room. She told me she had decided to convert to Judaism, but had not told my step son, Alan, yet as the date was still to be set and she was deciding on her Hebrew name with the Rabbi. This moment was an opening of her soul to mine, a gift that was intimate because of the gravity of this act, that as the mother, I was honored with this information and her willingness to open up to her authentic self to me. I will hold this experience dear and always remember it. Another experience that was most intimate moment of my life was the birth of my son. I was completely open, vulnerable, and afraid, but I trusted my doctor and my husband to guide me through my fear. I allowed myself the experience of bliss by enjoying the intimacy of a new life, of a birthing of a new chapter in my life, as well as the new life I was blessed by when I had Adam.

This week, open up to your true self, reflect on how and when you have been intimate with another person, and which shade of yourself was revealed in those moments. Realize who you really are and share it with the world.

Journal:

1) Use your journal to talk to that inner child. Becoming more intimate with yourself will help you to be more intimate with another.

2) So how do we get ready for intimacy? How do we learn the steps to openness? Look inside and ask when you have experienced this in your life. If the answer comes back "never" then begin to help yourself to create an open and intimate relationship with yourself. That's right! The inner work is where it begins; the inner child needs to feel safe.

3) Remember an intimate moment in your life and write in as much detail as possible so that you can bring up the feelings of that moment. This will help to cement the experience in your soul.

Books:

Intimate Connections by David Burns

David D Burns has contributed to Intimate Connections as an author, a clinical psychiatrist, conveys his ideas with warmth, compassion, understanding, and humor unmatched by any other writer in the self-help field.

The Dance of Intimacy by Harriet Learner

She is the bestselling author of *The Dance of Anger* and outlines the steps to take so that good relationships can be strengthened and difficult ones can be healed. Taking a careful look at those relationships where intimacy is most challenged–by distance, intensity, or pain–she teaches us about the specific changes we can make to achieve a more solid sense of self and a more intimate connectedness with others. Combining clear advice with vivid case examples, Dr. Lerner offers us the most solid, helpful book on intimate relationships that both women and men may ever encounter.

Films:

The Waking Life – Directed by Richard Linklater Starring: Ethan Hawke, Trevor Jack Brooks and Lorelei Linklater

A man shuffles through a dream meeting various people and discussing the meanings and purposes of the universe Dreams. What are they? An escape from reality or reality itself? Waking Life follows the dream(s) of one man and his attempt to find and discern the absolute difference between waking life and the dream world. While trying to figure out a way to wake up, he runs into many people on his way; some of which offer one sentence asides on life, others delving deeply into existential questions and life's mysteries. We become the main character. It becomes our dream and our questions being asked and answered. Can we control our dreams? What are they telling us about life? About death? About ourselves and where we come from and where we are going? The film does not answer all these for us. Instead, it inspires us to ask the questions and find the answers ourselves.

Casablanca directed by Michael Curtiz, starring Humphrey Bogart, Ingrid Bergman and Paul Henreid, and featuring Claude Rains, Conrad Veidt, Sydney Greenstreet, Peter Lorre and Dooley Wilson.

Set during World War II, it focuses on a man torn between, in the words of one character, love and virtue. He must choose between his love for a woman and helping her Czech Resistance leader husband escape from the Vichy-controlled Moroccan city of Casablanca to continue his fight against the Nazis.

Garden State written by, directed by, and starring Zach Braff, with Natalie Portman, Peter Sarsgaard, and Sir Ian Holm.

The film centers on Andrew Largeman (Braff), a 26-year-old actor/waiter who returns to his hometown in New Jersey after his mother dies. On his trip back, he meets a young woman by the name of Sam, who changes him in more ways than he could have ever imagined. In the end, due to their strong connection, Andrew decides to remain with Sam instead of flying back to Los Angeles to see where their relationship will go.

Journey

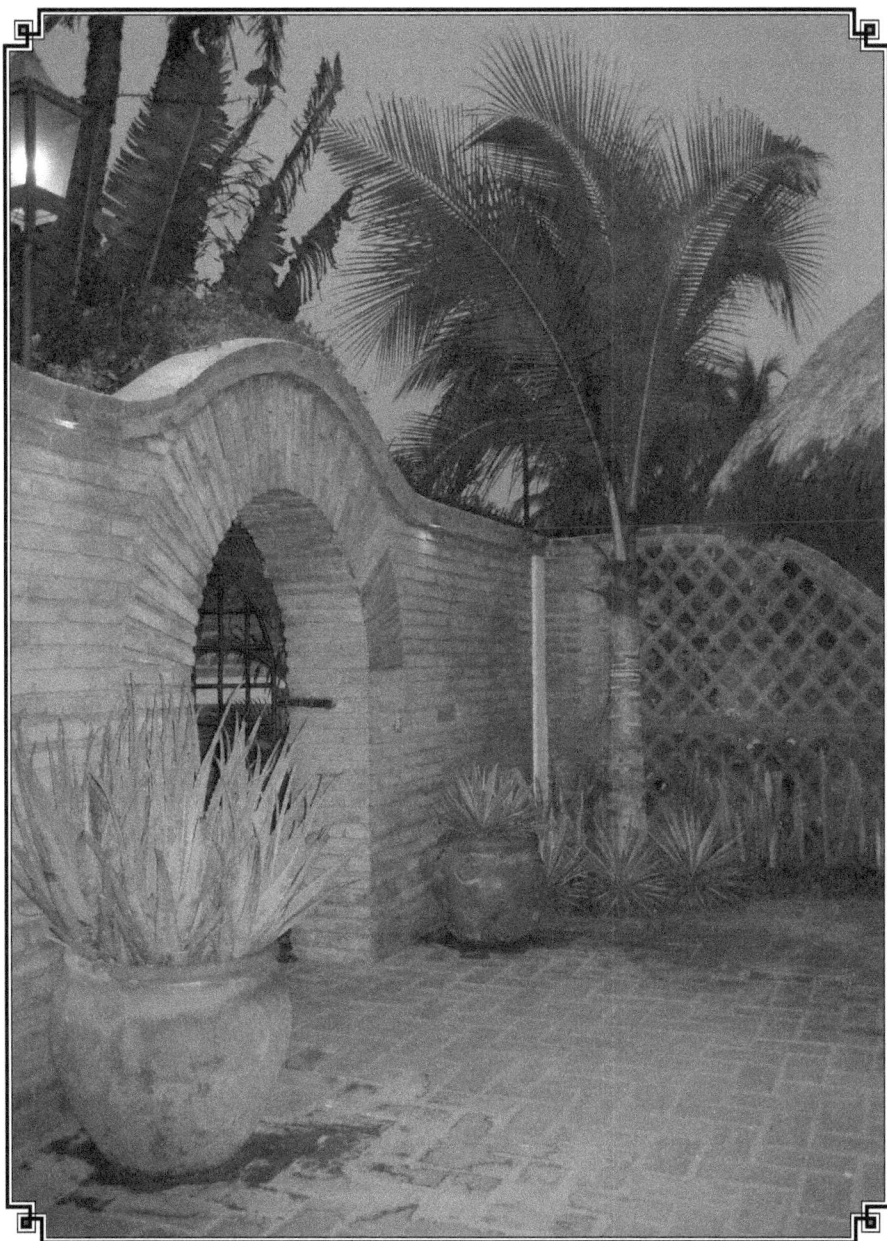

Journey

THE AUTHOR'S MEANING

A movement in which one creates
a process from start to finish

THE DICTIONARY DEFINITION

Journey is both a noun and a verb

- the act of traveling from one place to another verb

- undertake a journey or trip

- travel upon or across; travel the oceans;

> Twenty years from now you will be more disappointed
> by the things that you did not do than by the ones you did.
> So, throw off the bowlines. Sail away from the
> safe harbor; catch the trade winds
> in your sails.
>
> Explore, Dream, Discover......
>
> — Mark Twain

A JOURNEY ALWAYS BEGINS WITH THE FIRST STEP, WHETHER it is a physical one, such as a trip to Paris, or a spiritual one, like moving toward your authentic self. It is an experience that affects who we are and, at times, it can bring positive change into our lives. Some journeys reveal truths about our past, give us hope for the present, or allow us to discover new beginnings for our futures. On any journey one thing is clear: the process is more valuable to us than the first step, or even the last. It is the defining part of our quest to "live" while we take the trip.

One of my greatest journeys has been this book. From the first concept, the pen to paper, to the final word written on my iPad, the entire process spanned twelve years. This period has been everything from a dream to a struggle, but never dull. In my heart and mind I believe this book has importance for many people. That belief is the talisman to my motivation, propelling me to place one foot in front of the other and write. I had no idea of what the outcome of this book would be, let alone how the process would span out, but I knew I had to finish it. It tested my abilities, pushed my capabilities, and stressed my dedication to my project. Many of the struggles we face, the adventures we bound towards, or the obstacles we overcome, show the different strengths in our character and our hold on our beliefs. With each step it took to further its progress, this book reflects my journey to accomplish many of my goals in life. Completing this project was a symbol of my experiences and what I gained from them.

Like much of our lives, the journey must be completed to move on both physically and metaphorically. The gift of a journey is the experience and wisdom accumulated with each step, as it opens us to new information, allows us to attain our goals, and to strengthen our self-esteem. Throughout the journey we are challenged by fear and doubt, which stresses the importance of the process. When we overcome those obstacles, however, we overcome our questionings of self that hold us back. When we arrive at the final destination, we are filled with the knowledge that we can do anything we put our mind to accomplish.

Every journey in life has meaning and as we embark on many more of them, we will continue to grow. This week take a look at the different journeys you have embarked on physically and spiritually. Consider the changes in yourself that resulted from those experiences and how they affected you.

Journal:

1) What journeys have you embarked upon? Are they ones of adventure to far off places or an inner journey toward the real you? To enjoy the process of the journey is the true wisdom to life. This week I would suggest your introspection of past journeys such as vacations, business trips, pilgrimages and your learning's. Then reflect on your inner journeys i.e. seminars, meditations, gurus and the like. What was the most important part for you?

2) Taking the first step, creating the courage to go forward? Write down what you need to do to move forward on your journey. Think and pay attention to your thoughts; this will give you a perspective of who you are when it comes to "moving on"

3) Look around you and see what you can learn from other people's journeys. Look at those close to you, or at Buddha, Martha Stewart, Joan of Arc, Winston Churchill. Imagine what twists and turns took place in their lives and write it in your journal. It will give you another journey outside of yourself.

Books:

A Road Less Travelled *by M. Scott Peck*

Published in 1978 A Road Less Traveled is Peck's best-known work, and the one that made his reputation. It is, in short, a description of the attributes that make for a fulfilled human being, based largely on his experiences as a psychiatrist and a person. In the first section of the work Peck talks about discipline, which he considers essential for emotional, spiritual and psychological health, and which he describes as "the means of spiritual evolution". The elements of discipline that make for such health include the ability to delay gratification, accepting responsibility for oneself and one's actions, a dedication to truth and balancing.

In the second section, Peck considers the nature of *love*, which he considers the driving force behind spiritual growth. The section mainly attacks a number of misconceptions about love: that romantic love exists (he considers it a very destructive myth), that it is about dependency, that true love is the feeling of "falling in love". Instead, Peck argues that "true" love is about the extending of one's ego boundaries to include another, and about the spiritual nurturing of another.

December Sky: Beyond My Undocumented Life by Evelyn Cortez-Davis

Against all odds, Davis overcame these obstacles and earned an engineering degree from UCLA. Now, as a successful woman, she articulates skillfully about her experiences. What she faced growing up would have been daunting for anyone; but it was a journey for her that enabled her to grow and become the person that she is today. Despite some extremely scary moments where all of her hard work could have gone to waste, Evelyn stayed on track and learned quickly to use common sense to maneuver herself to safety. Her autobiography is definitely worth reading. It enabled me to view politics through the perspective of an individual who fought for her education and recognition as a successful Mexican-American woman.

No-No Boy by John Okada

No-No Boy is the only novel published by Japanese-American writer, John Okada. Set in 1946 in Seattle, Washington and written in the voice of an omniscient narrator who frequently blends into the voice of the protagonist, it is about one Japanese-American in the aftermath of the Japanese-American internment during World War II. Ichiro Yamada, former undergraduate at the University of Washington, returns home after two years in internment camp and two years in federal prison to the Japanese-American neighborhood south of downtown, where he wrestles with finding his place in society in the face of despising his parents and suffering occasional ostracism from his own community. The ostracism is because he had refused to join the United States armed forces. During the war, the government extended the offer to enlist to young male internees *en masse*. Few of them refused, and those who did were despised by many in the Japanese-American community, who bestowed on them the name "no-no boys". Yamada experiences inner turmoil as he tries to identify why things happened the way they did, why people hate one another, and why he made the choice he made.

Films:

Homeless to Harvard directed by Hollis McLachlan Starring Marcus Proctor

Thora Birch stars as Liz Murray, the homeless daughter of an extremely dysfunctional Bronx family. Liz is a young girl who is taken care of by her loving, but drug-addicted father and mother, who is also an alcoholic. After her mother dies of AIDS, which she got from sharing needles during her drug abuse, she got a 'slap in the face' by her mother's death and begins her work to finish high school, which she amazingly completed in two years, rather than the usual four. She becomes a star student and earns a scholarship to Harvard University through an essay contest sponsored by the New York Times.

127 Hours directed by Danny Boyle starring James Franco, Amber Tamblyn and Kate Mara

127 Hours is the true story of mountain climber Aron Ralston's remarkable adventure to save himself after a fallen boulder crashes on his arm and traps him in an isolated canyon in Utah. Over the next five days Ralston examines his life and survives the elements

to finally discover he has the courage and the wherewithal to extricate himself by any means necessary, scale a 65-foot wall and hike over eight miles before he can be rescued. Throughout his journey, Ralston recalls friends, lovers, family, and the two hikers he met before his accident. Will they be the last two people he ever had the chance to meet?

Knowledge

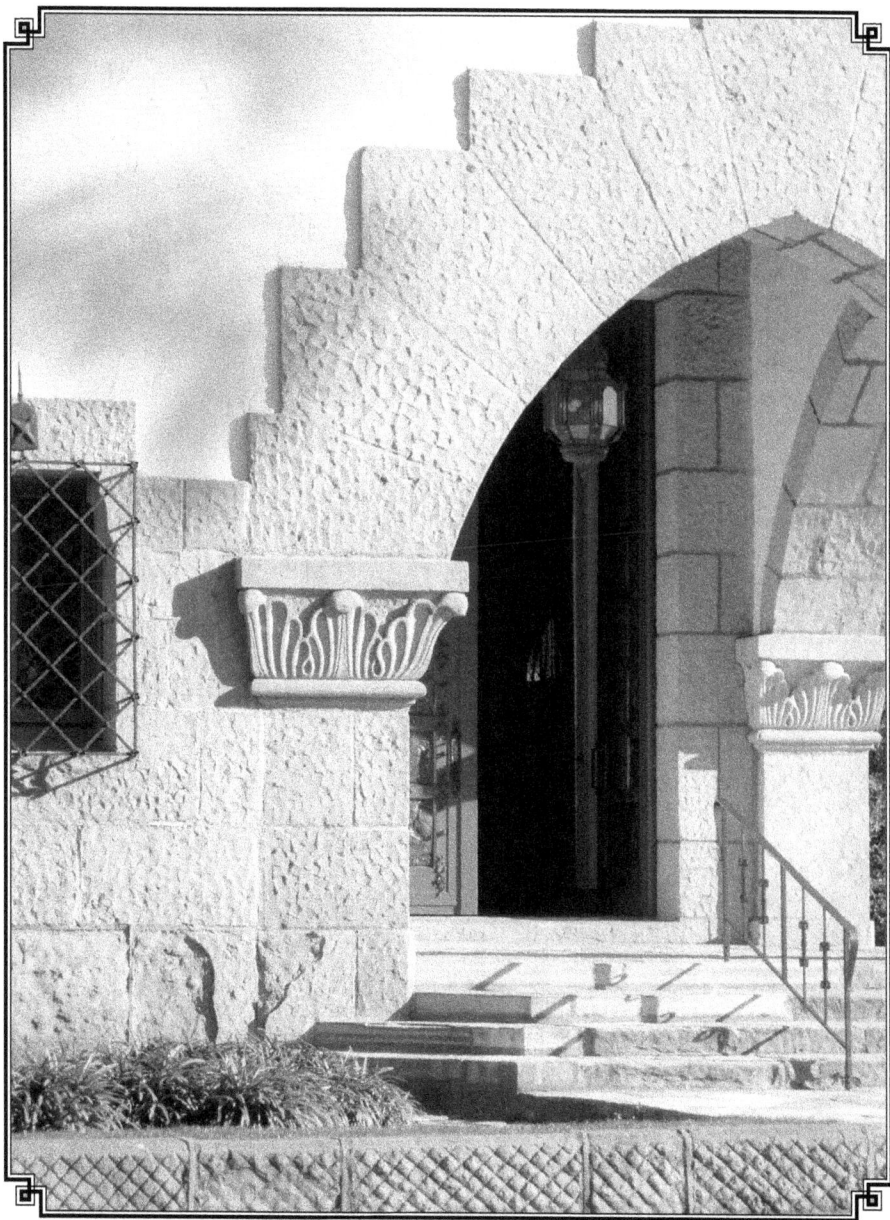

Knowledge

THE AUTHOR'S MEANING
Knowledge is a gathering of facts, ideas and perceptions

THE DICTIONARY DEFINITION
Knowledge is a noun

- the psychological result of perception and learning and reasoning

> The greater our knowledge increases,
> the greater our ignorance unfolds.
>
> — John F. Kennedy, Thirty-fifth President of the USA

KNOWLEDGE IS SUCH AN INTIMIDATING WORD TO ME AND can be difficult to write about. When I write about knowledge I fear that my readers will discover I do not know what I am talking about. Who am I to discuss the meaning of knowledge? Knowledge is information we obtain from what we hear, feel, and see. It is what we learn and what we experience, not limited to the textbooks we are forced to read in school or the way we interact with those around us. As a dyslexic child with terrible spelling and lack of an English degree, I always viewed myself as unintelligent; thus describing myself as *knowledgeable* was never in my vocabulary.

Things have certainly changed over time. In almost sixty years, I have obtained an amazing amount of knowledge. Knowledge is the gift given to us when we choose to ask, listen, look, read, and talk. It is everywhere and in everything. I once asked Diane Von Furstenberg, a Belgium-American fashion designer, how she became so successful in her life, and her words surprised me: "Pay attention to everything, that is what one does to gain knowledge." By being aware you become more knowledgeable because as you take in information, you recognize that there is valuable information in even the smallest details. That is not to say you will ever know everything or are necessarily intelligent, but with a little work we can all learn more.

I am a very proud grandma, my grandson, Clovis graduated from Berkley this year with a degree in Engineering Physics. His knowledge about this subject is at the highest level and he can use it in a number of ways. But I felt that the most important comments made at his graduation was that though the graduates had great knowledge in their field, it was their responsibility to leave the center and go towards the edge to create new thought, new ideas, new inventions for through knowledge great things can occur but you must look beyond what you think you know.

If we learn more, we can use our knowledge wisely to create better lives for ourselves and for the world. Knowledge is not specific to information you can obtain from an encyclopedia. It encompasses a variety of genres, like emotions, socialization, job skills, aesthetic abilities, and much more. Learning should be encouraged in all areas of our lives, and should be pursued beyond the textbooks. The knowledge we obtain can enrich our lives in ways that were unimaginable, bettering not only our conditions, but also even the conditions of those around us. Those who live ignorant and narrow lives are often the people who enjoy little and suffer more.

Consider the way you glean information, how you think about it, and sculpt it into knowledge. This is a gift, especially today when so much is available through the Internet, television, podcasts, and more. The ways to learn are endless, as well as the subjects to enlighten ourselves with. This week work to expand your knowledge by using different media sources in different interesting ways.

Journal:

1) Where do you get your knowledge? Do you ask questions of others? Do you look up information on the web? Have you ever thought about where you find what you need to make a decision? Please write this down in your journal and give it some thought.

2) Write down the areas of interest where you feel you have a great deal of knowledge, and areas where you lack knowledge and would like to pursue over time.

3) In your lifetime who has been the most knowledgeable person that you have met was it a teacher, parent, friend? When you know who it is write about their contribution to your life and what you will do with that knowledge.

Books:

Holler If You Hear Me: Searching for Tupac Shakur by Michael Eric Dyson

Ten years after his murder, Tupac Shakur is even more loved, contested, and celebrated than he was in life. His posthumously released albums, poetry, and motion pictures have catapulted him into the upper echelon of American cultural icons. In *Holler If You Hear Me*, "hip-hop intellectual" Michael Eric Dyson, acclaimed author of the bestselling *Is Bill Cosby Right?*, offers a wholly original way of looking at Tupac that will thrill those who already love the artist and enlighten those who want to understand him.

Dictionary of Cultural Literacy: What Every American Needs to Know by E. D. Hirsch, Joseph F. Kett

In this fast-paced information age, how can Americans know what's really important and what's just a passing fashion? Now more than ever, we need a source that concisely sums up the knowledge that matters to Americans – the people, places, ideas, and events that shape our cultural conversation. With more than six thousand entries the New Dictionary of Cultural Literacy is that invaluable source.

Atlas Shrugged by Ayn Rand

First published in 1957 in the United States. Rand's fourth and last novel, it was also her longest, and the one she considered to be her *magnum opus* in the realm of fiction writing. *Atlas Shrugged* includes elements of romance, mystery and science fiction, and it contains Rand's most extensive statement of Objectivism in any of her works of fiction. The theme of *Atlas Shrugged*, as Rand described it, is "the role of man's mind in existence". The book explores a number of philosophical themes that Rand would subsequently develop into the philosophy of Objectivism. It advocates the core tenets of Rand's philosophy of Objectivism and expresses her concept of human achievement. In doing so, it expresses many facets of Rand's philosophy, such as the advocacy of reason, individualism, capitalism, and the failures of government coercion.

Films:

Good Will Hunting directed by Gus Van Sant Starring Matt Damon, Robin Williams, Ben Affleck, Minnie Driver, and Stellan Skarsgård. Written by Affleck and Damon

Will Hunting, a janitor at MIT, has a gift for mathematics but needs help from a psychologist to find direction in his life. With Damon in the title role, the film follows 20-year-old South Boston laborer Will Hunting, a genius that is forced to see a therapist and study advanced mathematics with a renowned professor in order to avoid jail time. Through his therapy sessions, Will re-evaluates his relationships with his best friend (Affleck) and his girlfriend (Driver) while confronting his emotional issues and making decisions about his future.

Crash directed by Paul Haggis with Don Cheadle and Sandra Bullock

The film is about racial and social tensions in Los Angeles, California. Several characters' stories interweave during two days in Los Angeles: a black LAPD detective estranged from his mother; his criminal younger brother and gang associate; the white District Attorney and his irritated and pampered wife; a racist white police officer who disgusts his more idealistic younger partner; an African American Hollywood director and his wife who must deal with the officer; a Persian-immigrant father who is wary of others; and a Hispanic locksmith. The film differs from many other films about racism in its rather impartial approach to the issue. Rather than separating the characters into victims and offenders, victims of racism are often shown to be racist themselves in different contexts and situations. Also, racist remarks and actions are often shown to stem from ignorance and misconception rather than a malicious personality.

Laughter

Laughter

The medicine of joy that heals through release

THE DICTIONARY DEFINITION
Laughter is a noun

- the sound of laughing; he enjoyed the laughter of the crowd;

- the activity of laughing; the manifestation of joy or mirth of scorn;

- to show mirth, joy, or scorn with a Smile and chuckle or explosive sound

> Laughter – An interior convulsion, producing a distortion of the features and accompanied by inarticulate noises. It is infectious and, though intermittent, incurable.
>
> — Ambrose Bierce

LAUGHTER IS A VIBRATION THAT UPLIFTS OUR BEING, AND a medicine of joy that heals the world through its release. It is an act of our bodies, a physical response that is the same for every individual. When we laugh our insides are massaged, our faces relax, and the sound permeates through the world around us. This simple, automatic act helps us put our emotions and thoughts into a lighter perspective. It seems like such a trivial response, but laughter brings so much into our lives. Think of when we laugh in times of joy, embarrassment, or fear. All these moments express a degree of vulnerability, and with laughter, we are provided an escape. It is a necessary release that is available to everyone. Laughter is a very special ingredient of life because it is able to change us in every way.

Laughing is a form of communication. It is a way to connect to the people, and the world, that surround us. Laughing is a mechanism allowing our minds to establish that we are not alone in what we do. It is a way to secure us in a comfortable environment and accept ourselves. We laugh when we trip on a rock, fall down a flight of stairs, or when we drop our ice cream cone. All these situations evoke negative feelings, but the result of our laughter diminishes the threats that cloud our minds, or the fear we may begrudgingly succumb to. Laughter is also a form of positive communication. We laugh when we smile, love, and surround ourselves in complete happiness. Laughter is a key to embracing our circumstances and overcoming the difficulties we may face.

When I was going through my long illness I read *Anatomy of an Illness* by Norman Cousins. He stated that laughter could heal, and he was right. When I watch a funny movie, I do feel better. When a laugh escapes my body, I am overcome with joy. Have you noticed how wonderful you feel after a good laugh? I always felt the relationships that flourish and sustain me are those in which I laugh often. Those individuals are the ones who make my life enjoyable and remind me of our connection. Laughter is a symbol of the happiness we can all call forth no matter the circumstances we find ourselves in. It is a tool to fix your attitude and change the outcome of any situation.

When we laugh we accept, we enjoy, and we see past what was threatening. It is medicine to our psyche, a band-aid to any broken heart, and a cure to any sadness. Laughing a little more each day can bring a smile to our faces when we least expect it.

This week, focus on the impact laughter has on your life and try to do more of it.

Journal:

1. Rent a movie, read a funny book. Have you thought about how you bring laughter into your life? This week's prescription is a laugh tonic three times a day. Enjoy the week.

2. When do you remember first laughing? Was it when you watched Sesame Street? Or when your mom pushed you on the swing? Think back to childhood joy and write the memories down.

3. Try to just laugh out loud! For no other reason but to move your energy, your face and your internal organs. Try it for two minutes and you will be amazed at how you feel.

Books:

Junie B. Jones by Barbara Park and illustrated by Denise Brunkus.

The story is written from Junie B.'s perspective. Juniper Beatrice "Junie B." Jones The series' title character and main protagonist, Junie B., lives with her parents and her baby brother, Ollie. All of the books in the series describe her candid adventures through kindergarten and first grade, and are sure to pack in a good laugh. She is a curious and honest child, and the actions she often makes using her best judgments drive the adults around her insane. In addition to giving me a good laugh, reading her books made me take a second look at what I take seriously in my life and if each of those things are worth worrying about.

Dress Your Family in Corduroy and Denim by David Sedaris

David Sedaris returns to his deliriously twisted domain: hilarious childhood dramas infused with melancholy; the gulf of misunderstanding that exists between people of different nations or members of the same family; and the poignant divide between one's best hopes and most common deeds. The family characters his readers love are all here, as well as the unique terrain.

Films:

Patch Adams directed by Tom Shadyac with Robin Williams, Daniel London

Laughter is the Best Medicine – this is the motto of Dr. Patch Adams. After trying to commit suicide, Adams enrolls in medical school. Although he is older than most students, he has the uncanny ability to master all concepts while studying minimally. He maintains an eternally optimistic attitude that is contagious to everyone around him; Adams has the gift of being able to connect with everyone and make them laugh.

Although is sense of humor lands him in trouble because it goes against the grain of traditional hard-science doctors, the patients' conditions seem to improve with Adams' presence. This movie was made after the real Dr. Patch Adams, who is 67 today.

Mr. Bean's Holiday directed by Steven Bendelack with Rowan Atkinson

This is a movie that will make you laugh until your sides ache! Rowan Atkinson stars as Mr. Bean who is taking a vacation in Cannes. Along the way, his painfully clumsy nature lands him in the most interesting situations – some which work to his benefit, and others not so much. Through it all, he maintains his sense of humor and stays focused on the goal: get to Cannes. His relentless drive, even in the face of a hundred potential setbacks, makes for a great adventure in finally reaching Cannes.

Blazing Saddles directed by Mel Brooks with Gene Wilder, Cleavon Little, Slim Pickens

Mel Brooks was on a roll in the late-'60s and '70s with a string of intermittently hilarious spoofs, from 'The Producers' to 'Silent Movie'. In between, in 1974, he wrote and helmed this mostly very funny western send-up starring regular Gene Wilder. It's a typically bizarre close-to-the-bone scenario: with a view to procuring their land, a local swindler tries to shock the residents into leaving by organizing the employment of a new sheriff. It looks like his ruse might work when a clean-cut black man rides in to take the job... Brooks doesn't shy away from the race issue; in fact, he charges straight in with a sarcastic and very amusing sideswipe at bigotry and ignorance. There are so many cracking scenes to savor, but for me the most memorable sequence by far is that unique, sprawling ending when the whole cast of hundreds spills over into the movie lot. Brilliant.

Money

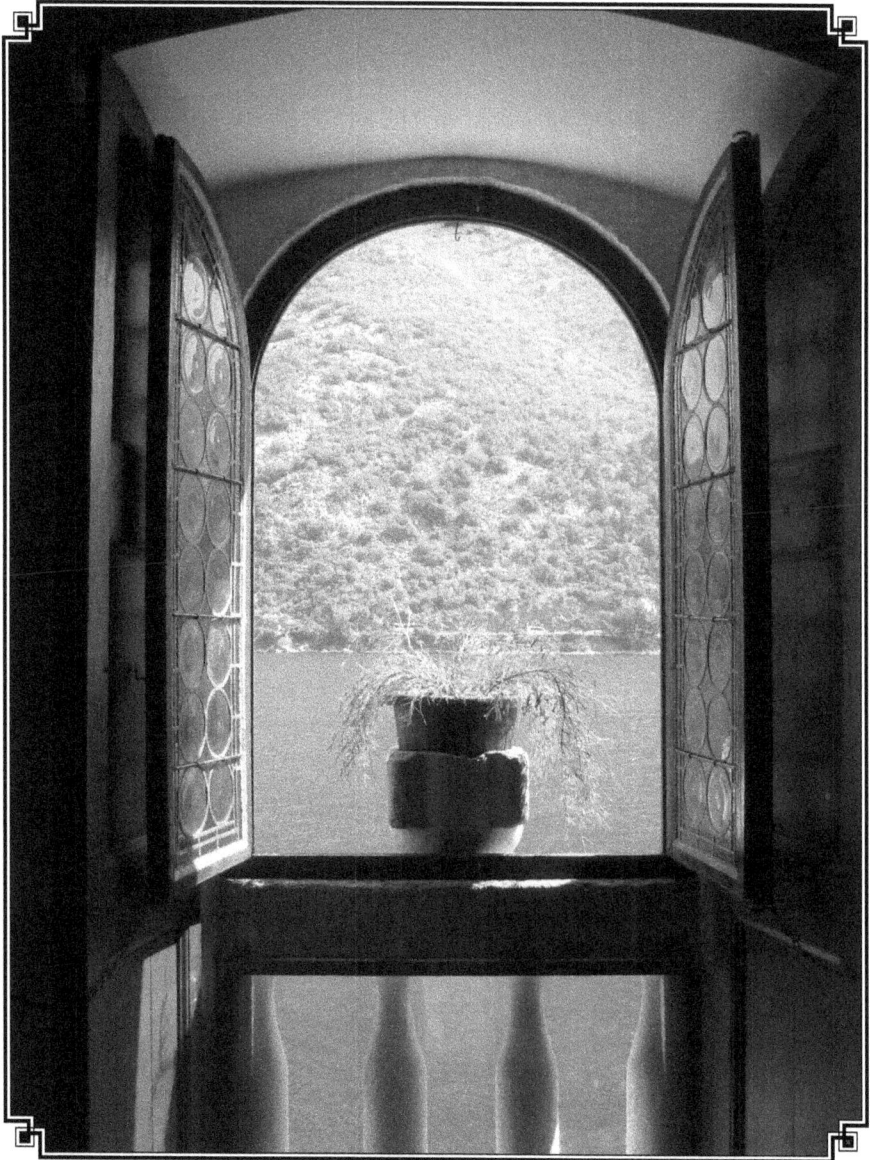

Money

*Money is the physical energy that
circulates around the planet*

THE DICTIONARY DEFINITION
Money is a noun

- the most common medium of exchange; functions as legal tender; we tried to collect the money he owed us; he changed his money into francs;

- wealth reckoned in terms of money; all his money is in real estate;

- the official currency issued by a government or national bank;

Money is the most important thing in the world.
It represents health, strength, honor, generosity, and beauty as conspicuously as the want of it represents illness, weakness, disgrace, meanness, and ugliness.

— George Bernard Shaw

MONEY MAKES THE WORLD GO AROUND. MONEY IS THE source of all evil. Money, money, money. This is a subject we spend much time in our lives thinking about. How do we make it? How do we keep it? Do we deserve it?

Money is the one area of life that affects almost every other area of our lives. It makes a difference on where we live, go to school, and what clothes and foods we choose to buy. It also affects our health care and our ability to do what we want, when we want. For many of us it creates an underlying fear we carry around and can overshadow different parts of our lives. It is the financial capital we need to make most of our dreams a reality, but it can also be the green goblin pushing us toward greed. In these contexts, money can be both liberating and limiting.

What wisdom have I learned about money? It is energy. Money is a substance that gives us sustenance, no more and no less. It is important that we make peace with our lack or abundance of it. Obsessing about our financial standing can bring pain and create struggles between friendships and family ties. On the other hand, understanding its function in your life can give you freedom and joy.

As we decide on our way of obtaining money with a job or a career, we often base the decision solely on what we hope to earn. On the contrary, I think the decision should be based on what makes us feel fulfilled, happy, and on actions that will be reflect our authentic selves. Then, and only then, we can choose a field of interest that allows us to be rich in accomplishment and peace of mind while the money follows. It is a way to enhance our lives economically and personally.

My personal story this week is about my mother's perspective on money and the way she gave me the sense of acceptance about its meaning. My mother told me money is to be used, to circulate, which is why it is called currency: it is a current like the ocean. She told me that if we used it properly we would always be cared for. My mother believed that if you only have five dollars in your pocket, you have more than a woman on the streets with nothing, so give it to her and more money will find its way to you. I have always found this to be true. Instead of fearing the loss of money, the intent of giving will fill the trough, and the money will circulate back. This is not a scientific finding, nor one that an economist might agree with, but it has always worked in my life. I respect the need for money but I also understand its simplicity. It is only money, and there are other things that matter much more in my life. My family, my friends, my health, the environment, and our planet all need money. They are as significant as the importance we give them.

This week examine your relationship to money. How deep is your need for it? Do you give more than you get, or vise versa? Consider the ways you can circulate money in your life and how you manage the income that flows to you.

Journal:

1) My exercise for you this week is to write down everything you spend. I mean everything from a pack of gum to your rent. Create a budget and be honest with yourself. Money can be saved, spent, won or lost by the decisions you make.

2) What did your family tell you about the importance of money? Do you have fear around it or do you need it to feel fulfilled? What is your feeling when you think of money?

3) How can you create additional money in your life? Do you have enough? If not why, and what can you do about it?

Books:

First Comes Love, Then Comes Money by Bethany and Scott Palmer

Bethany and Scott Palmer, "the money couple", have a combined 35 years of financial planning experience. Their extensive experience chronicles the pitfalls of money dishonesty between couples and what to do about this grave chasm of trust. If you are in a relationship, read this book and circumvent the travails of money mismatches.

Money is a symptom of underlying marital problems especially for young couples in their 20s, embarking on new projects and life decisions. To avoid money infidelity couples must practice healthy communication.

Money attitudes affect every decision we make. This solution-oriented approach helps the reader not only define and understand the problem, but offers actionable solutions to prevent and solve couple's money problems.

The book is filled with colorful anecdotes and stories illustrating the devastating problems of money and relationships.

The Richest Man In Babylon by George Samuel Clason

The Richest Man in Babylon is a book that dispenses financial advice through a collection of parables set in ancient Babylon. Through their experiences in business and managing household finance, the characters in the parables learn simple lessons in financial wisdom. Originally, a series of separate informational pamphlets distributed by banks and insurance companies, the pamphlets were bound together and published in book form in 1926.

The Soul of Money by Lynne Twist

This unique and fundamentally liberating book shows us that examining our attitudes toward money—earning it, spending it, and giving it away—can offer surprising insight into our lives, our values, and the essence of prosperity. Lynne Twist, a global activist and fundraiser, has raised more than $150 million for charitable causes. Through personal stories and practical advice, she demonstrates how we can replace feelings of scarcity, guilt, and burden with experiences of sufficiency, freedom, and purpose. In this

Nautilus Award-winning book, Twist shares from her own life, a journey illuminated by remarkable encounters with the richest and poorest, from the famous (Mother Teresa and the Dalai Lama) to the anonymous but unforgettable heroes of everyday life. "An inspired, utterly fascinating book. "A book for everyone who would like to make the world a better place." Jane Goodall.

The Money Book for the Young, Fabulous & Broke
by Suze Orman

This book is financial expert Suze Orman's answer to a generation's cry for help. They're called "Generation Debt" and "Generation Broke" by the media — people in their twenties and thirties who graduate college with a mountain of student loan debt and are stuck with one of the weakest job markets in recent history. The goals of their parents' generation — buy a house, support a family, send kids to college, retire in style — seem absurdly, depressingly out of reach. They live off their credit cards, may or may not have health insurance, and come up so far short at the end of the month that the idea of saving money is a joke. This generation has it tough, without a doubt, but they're also painfully aware of the urgent need to take matters into their own hands.

The Complete Idiot's Guide to Managing Your Money, 4th Edition

Expert financial columnist Robert K. Heady and financial writer Christy Heady take readers step-by-step through the process of getting their finances under control. With new, updated content for today's post-boom, cautious climate, this author team gives readers the knowledge they need to succeed. New content includes expanded and updated coverage on debt and expense management; updated and additional information on financial law; and up-to-date data based on forecasts, trends, and projected economic recovery.

Films:

Money Ball directed by Bennett Miller with Brad Pitt, Robin Wright & Jonah Hill

The central premise of Moneyball is that the collected wisdom of baseball insiders (including players, managers, coaches, scouts, and the front office) over the past century is subjective and often flawed. Statistics such as stolen bases, runs batted in, and batting average, typically used to gauge players, are relics of a 19th century view of the game and the statistics that were available at the time. The book argues that the Oakland A's' front office took advantage of more analytical gauges of player performance to field a team that could compete successfully against richer competitors in Major League Baseball (MLB). Rigorous statistical analysis had demonstrated that on-base percentage and slugging percentage are better indicators of offensive success, and the A's became convinced that these qualities were cheaper to obtain on the open market than more historically valued qualities such as speed and contact.

Wall Street directed by Oliver Stone and stars Michael Douglas, Charlie Sheen, and Daryl Hannah.

The film tells the story of Bud Fox (Sheen), a young stockbroker desperate to succeed who becomes involved with his hero, Gordon Gekko (Douglas), a wealthy, unscrupulous corporate raider. Stone made the film as a tribute to his father, Lou Stone, a stockbroker during the Great Depression. The character of Gekko is said to be a composite of several people, including Owen Morrisey, Dennis Levine, Ivan Boesky, Carl Icahn, Asher Edelman, Michael Ovitz, Michael Milken, and Stone himself. The character of Sir Lawrence Wildman, meanwhile, was modeled on the prominent British financier and corporate raider Sir James Goldsmith.

The Corporation directed by Jennifer Abbott, Mark Achbar

This documentary explains how corporations are the dominant institution of our lifetimes. They tell us what is good, what is bad; what to shop for and where to get it; what constitutes a "rich" lifestyle or a "poor" one. Additionally, the film talks about large corporations and how their economic incentives to continue business come before the acknowledgement of plundering the environment. Until the environment itself becomes an economic commodity, CEOs and big companies will not turn their attention to it. The greed for money will eventually cause so much environmental degradation that the products companies sell will become trivial concerns when our living conditions become threatened.

Nature

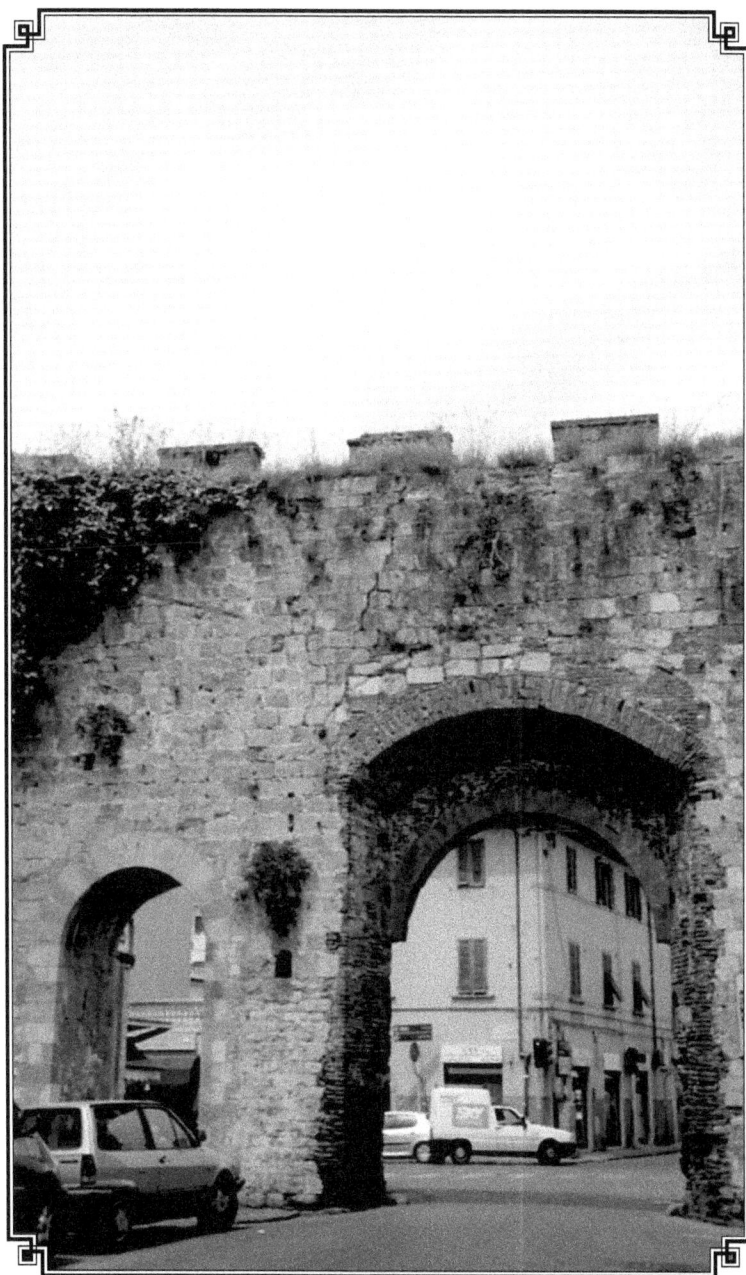

Nature

THE AUTHOR'S MEANING
Nature is the expression of all living things

THE DICTIONARY DEFINITION
Nature is a noun

- the essential qualities or characteristics by which something is recognized; it is the nature of fire to burn; the true nature of jealousy; the laws of nature; nature has seen to it that men are stronger than women; they tried to preserve nature as they found it; it is his nature to help others;

- a causal agent creating and controlling things in the universe;

- the natural physical world including plants and animals and landscapes etc;

- the complex of emotional and intellectual attributes that determine a person's characteristic actions and reactions;

- a particular type of thing; problems of this type are very difficult to solve; he's interested in trains and things of that nature; matters of a personal nature;

> When one tugs at a single thing in nature,
> he finds it attached to the rest of the world....
>
> — John Muir

THE WORLD HOLDS MUCH MEANING THAT IS SHOWN IN different forms in the physical environment and our personas. The most obvious one is the expression of the earth through the animals, plants, and all living things surrounding us. Let us put focus on the tangible first. Nature is a place where we find solace, calm, quiet, and beauty. It is captured in the magic of a snow covered pine forest, or the dance of fish as they swim through a babbling brook. It can be found in the joy of a fawn on wobbling legs, opening its eyes as it takes its first steps. The physical environment is continuously examined to interpret its importance and is cherished by individuals who seek comfort from it. The physical environment is an aesthetic expression of life.

Nature portrays perfection in its balance. It balances itself with its inhabitants through the cycle of predator and prey, and it cleanses itself with the cycle of rain. The physical environment can be viewed as a perfect system creating a constant process of life. This is one meaning of the word, which I suggest you think upon.

The second meaning is the defining element of our character. Human nature in many ways is opposed to the general translation of the word. What is human nature? Is it our nature to create war, control our environments, and overpower our enemies through wars, economic injustice, and cruelty? Or can our nature be composed of compassion, charity, and love? I believe we are like the general form of nature, a balance in itself and of it all. There are two sides to human nature; in the same way there are two sides to a coin. Both opposing elements exist within us, but how we choose to act on them compose our characters.

I often find myself asking, "how can we make this a better world, and who is balancing the world through their work?" When I ponder on this thought, my mind directs itself to the lives of Mahatma Gandhi, Mother Teresa, Jane Goodall, Mohammed Yunis, Barbara Marx Hubbard, and hundreds of individuals who like them, worked to innovate change in the world they lived in. Their nature led the world to establish answers to our problems and to evoke compassionate understandings of human kind. They are the visionaries who, to this very day, show humanity the greatness and potential of human nature. Although our nature is flawed, it does not enforce us to succumb to the darkest of inhibitions.

This week take the time to interpret your nature and your interactions with the environment around you. Consider the different ways you appreciate the environment and your own character. Focus on the betterment of your surroundings to reform your relationship with the environment and yourself.

Journal:

1) Make a list of the things in nature that bring you joy, solace, relaxation and focus. Imagine being in that place and envision the feelings it brings to you.

2) Consider the people whose nature inspires you and gives you the sense of being in your highest nature, in what way do you see your nature? How do you conduct your life and where do you separate nature and consciousness in the human being?

3) Where do you experience the most awe for the beauty of the place, in the world of nature? For me it is next to a gentle river, falling over rocks, sitting on the bank in the grass and watching the leaves above in the sycamore trees shimmer as the sun reflects a constant glimmer of light. The smell is of the grass, the river and the drying leaves a cacophony of senses not the least of which is the feeling of the sun on my skin with the breeze cooling it with every breath. This is my secret place where nature provides me with grace and peace. Do you have such a place that you can create at any time you like and meditate on its grandeur, beauty, and grounding essence?

Books:

Silent Spring by Rachel Carson

The book argued that uncontrolled and unexamined pesticide use was harming and even killing not only animals and birds, but also humans. Its title was meant to evoke a spring season in which no bird songs could be heard, because they had all vanished as a result of pesticide abuse. The book documented detrimental effects of pesticides on the environment and particularly on birds. Carson accused the chemical industry of spreading disinformation, and public officials of accepting industry claims uncritically.

Earth Odyssey by Michael Hertsgaard

Like many of us, Mark Hertsgaard has long worried about the declining health of our environment. But in 1991, he decided to act on his own concern and investigate the escalating crisis for himself. Traveling on his own dime, he embarked on an odyssey lasting most of the decade and spanning nineteen countries. Now, in Earth Odyssey he reports on our environmental predicament through the eyes of the people who live it. Earth Odyssey is a vivid, passionate narrative about one man's journey around the world in search of the answer to the essential question of our time: Is the future of the human species at risk? Combining first-rate reportage with irresistible storytelling, Mark Hertsgaard has written an essential–and ultimately hopeful–book about the uncertain fate of humankind.

Films:

Ferngully: The Last Rainforest directed by Bill Kroyer with Samantha Mathis, Robin Williams & Christian Slater

In this movie about nature, Crysta is a fairy that, with the help of a human, has to save the rainforest from Hexus, a creature of pollution and destruction. Not only does this movie teach a great lesson about protecting rainforests, but it also has Robin Williams doing the voice of the amusing Batty Koda and Tim Curry voicing Hexus with his deep, evil voice.

March of the Penguins directed by Luc Jacquet with Morgan Freeman

Let's face it: the penguins are cute. This documentary became a huge hit in the US with its story about penguin life and love. It is a movie about nature, real nature that struck a cord with everyone and even spawned several spoofs. Not only does it teach us about penguin life, but it also discusses the effect of global warming

Oceans directed by Jacques Perrin distributed in the United States by Disneynature.

It was released on April 22, 2010 in 1,200 theaters in the US for Earth Day. The film explores Earth's five oceans. Budgeted at 50 million Euros ($66 million US), it was filmed in over 50 different places and took four years to film. The movie is a high-quality filming documentary featuring ocean animals. It reflects the need to respect nature and demonstrates the negative aspects of human activity on animals.

Oneness

Oneness

Oneness is the experience we have when we see our connection to everything

THE DICTIONARY DEFINITION
Oneness is a noun

- singleness; unity

- unity of mind, feeling, or purpose

- sameness; identity

> "Wisdom is your perspective on life, your sense of balance, your understanding of how the various parts and principles apply and relate to each other. It embraces judgment, discernment and comprehension. It is a gestalt or oneness, and integrated wholeness
>
> — Stephen R. Covey

ONENESS IS WHOLENESS, UNITY, AND THE VERY ESSENCE OF the universe. The oneness we live in is breathtaking. My son Adam once expressed the idea that an entire universe could exist within each particle of dust. He was seven years old when he delivered this proclamation of everyone being connected. He was lying down in our hallway looking up at the light pouring through the window, making specs of dust dance and flow in the air surrounding it. He invited me to lay down with him and see what he saw, feel what he felt, and think what he thought. In those moments our thoughts were connected and I understood what he was saying. It put my thoughts into words.

Scientists in many fields throughout the world examine such a connection between thought and matter. We are all connected through our DNA, through the stuff of the big bang, through all that is and all that will ever be. We are all part of the oneness of life. Though this may sound surreal, it is not. It is what the spiritual leaders have always said, what the scientists continue to look into. It is all a matter of how we are connected and to what! This is important in understanding that a conscious evolution is the way to a new paradigm for our world.

Oneness can often begin from within the small place inside our heads where the tiny voice is heard, where we go to find solace or peace. Oneness can be felt when you meditate because in that place infinity exists which is the oneness of being. It is the understanding of our connection to our surroundings, and to one another.

This week acknowledge the feelings that make you feel a bond to what is around you and take the time to discover your connection to other individuals. This unity is the backbone of what it means to be human and brings us together.

Journal:

1) What do you feel is the one thing that unites you to the whole? Is it God, nature, the Internet, meditation, thought, prayer, family, what is your connection?

2) Is the fact that we think about something enough of an impetus to drive the others who think like us to create an oneness? Look up the "The Hundredth Monkey" effect on Wikipedia and see what I mean.

3) Who in your world do you think has the most understanding of this principle? Can you ask for a meeting with your clergy, a professor, or a friend? Think of whom you might discuss this with and go talk to them, then write down what you learned.

Books:

Walden written by noted transcendentalist Henry David Thoreau.

The work is part personal declaration of independence, social experiment, voyage of spiritual discovery, satire, and manual for self-reliance. Published in 1854, it details Thoreau's experiences over the course of two years in a cabin he built near Walden Pond, amidst woodland owned by his friend and mentor Ralph Waldo Emerson, near Concord, Massachusetts. By immersing himself in nature, Thoreau hoped to gain a more objective understanding of society through personal introspection. Simple living and self-sufficiency were Thoreau's other goals, and the whole project was inspired by transcendentalist philosophy, a central theme of the American Romantic Period. As Thoreau made clear in his book, his cabin was not in wilderness but at the edge of town, about two miles (3 km) from his family home.

Leviathan by Thomas Hobbes

Its name derives from the biblical Leviathan. The work concerns the structure of society and legitimate government, and is regarded as one of the earliest and most influential examples of social contract theory. In *Leviathan*, which was written during the English Civil War (1642–1651), Hobbes argues for a social contract and rule by an absolute sovereign. He wrote that chaos or civil war – situations identified with a state of nature and the famous motto *Bellum omnium contra omnes* ("the war of all against all") – could only be averted by strong central government.

Birth 2012 and Beyond written by Barbara Marx Hubbard.

She is an author, public speaker, social innovator, and president of the Foundation for Conscious Evolution. She has initiated a guided educational program supported by Internet systems called *Gateway to Conscious Evolution*, offering a new developmental path toward the next stage of human evolution, now reaching over 1000 people. She is creating a new vehicle, The Communion of Pioneering Souls, to connect the large group of evolving humans now arising in every culture, field, and tradition. She is developing a new series of videos entitled "Humanity Ascending: A New Way through Together."

Films:

I AM directed by Tom Shadyac

I AM is an utterly engaging and entertaining non-fiction film that poses two practical and provocative questions: what's wrong with our world, and what can we do to make it better? The filmmaker behind the inquiry is Tom Shadyac, one of Hollywood's leading comedy practitioners and the creative force behind such blockbusters as "Ace Ventura," "Liar Liar," "The Nutty Professor," and "Bruce Almighty." However, in I AM, Shadyac steps in front of the camera to recount what happened to him after a cycling accident left him incapacitated, possibly for good. Though he ultimately recovered, he emerged with a new sense of purpose, determined to share his own awakening to his prior life of excess and greed, and to investigate how he as an individual, and we as a race, could improve the way we live and walk in the world.

The Celestine Prophecy by James Redfield

Its nine key insights predict a worldwide awakening, arising within all religious traditions, that moves humanity toward a deeper experience of spirituality. Based on James Redfield's worldwide best-selling novel, The Celestine Prophecy is a spiritual adventure film chronicling the discovery of ancient scrolls in the rain forests of Peru. "If we pay attention, we can find a greater life, no matter where we are, no matter who we are, no matter what our circumstances are. If you tune into the mysterious coincidences in your life, if you discover and then follow your intuitions, you will find that there's a door of opportunity for a greater life for you. You can't be a victim and do it, but if you go beyond that, if you find a way out of whatever circumstance you're in, whatever block you think you might face, what happens is that it works. It always works. The only thing that holds any of us back is not believing that it works."

Passion

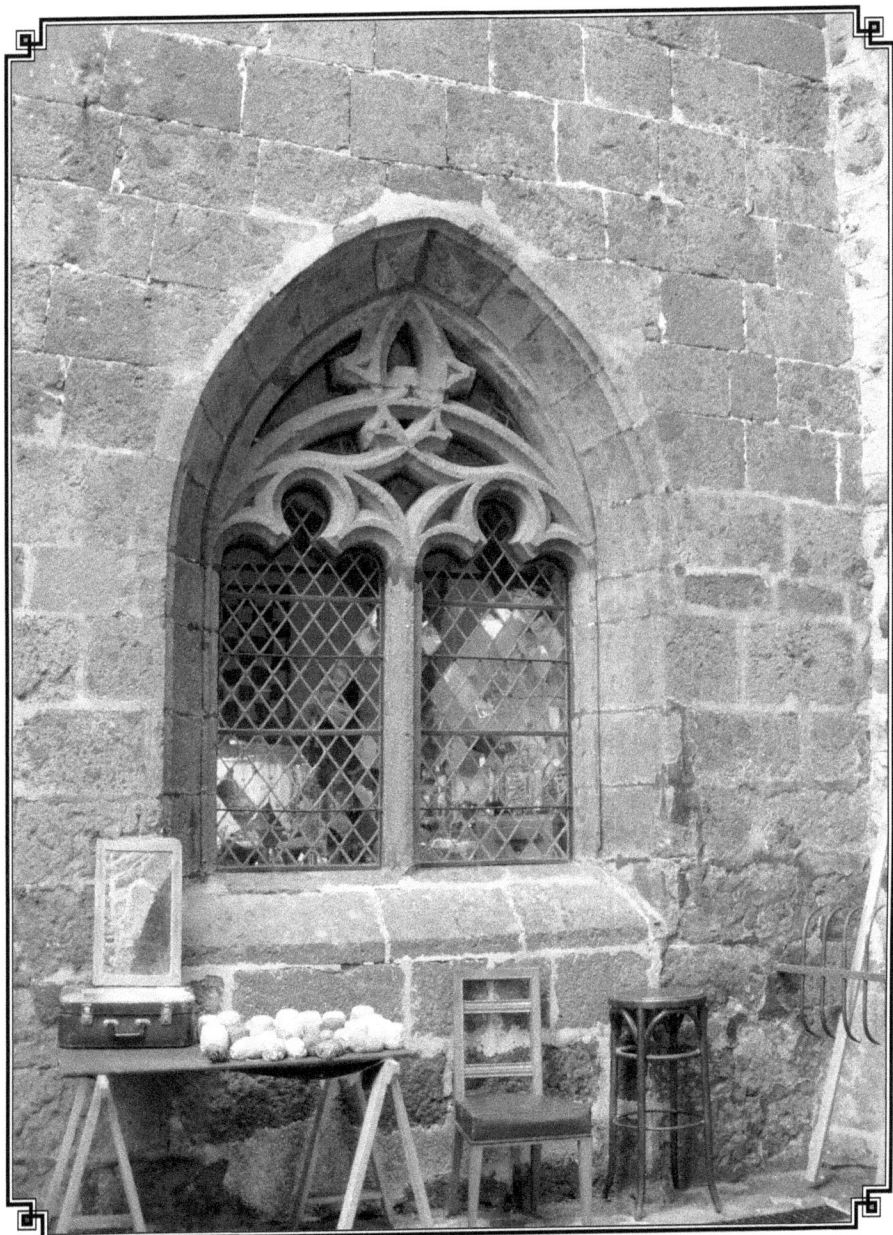

Passion

THE AUTHOR'S MEANING
Passion is the juice of life

THE DICTIONARY DEFINITION
Passion is a noun

- strong feeling or emotion

- intense passion or emotion

- something that is desired intensely; his rage for fame destroyed him;

- an irrational but irresistible motive for a belief or action

- a feeling of strong sexual desire

- any object of warm affection or devotion; the theater was her first love; he has a passion for cock fighting;

- the suffering of Jesus at the crucifixion

> We may affirm absolutely that nothing great in the world has been accomplished without passion.
>
> — Hegel

PASSION IS MY FAVORITE WORD BECAUSE IT IS FILLED WITH Life. Passion is a gift. Not to say passion makes life easy, it does not, but it makes it lively. When I carve stone I feel passion, passion for the stone, the work, the result, and the art of it all. I often have a sense of being out of control when I am in the midst of passion. Passion leads us into a place where we rarely feel ourselves. We feel a focus on the desire and it fuels a fire in our mind, body, and soul. The passion takes us over as if to burn us up. Impassioned is where we have the essence of insanity close in on us. Think about the great minds of Galileo, Gandhi, MLK, and Tupac, whom society condemned because they went against the grain to follow their passions. They are now praised and admired because they were committed and dedicated to their passions.

Unfortunately, like all things in life there is always another side to every coin. Even as passion can blossom into a light of life, it can just as easily spiral into an all-consuming evil. It can stir individuals into a darker side of life and they can succumb to hate and wicked crimes. For example, there are the passionate haters, people who murdered for passion, or the passionate dare devil that lost his life because he was not using his brain, just his passion. These occurrences are a result of a dark passion, one that is more destructive than enriching.

I can remember a day when I was overtaken by passion. I was carving and sanding a piece of stone to create a sculpture, I worked for hours and hours, and by the end of the day I was bleeding, my face was sandblasted raw and I fell to the ground exhausted. The piece of work was one of my best ever, but it took me days to recover. I was filled with so much passion for the work that I lost sight of the physical toll it took on me.

My point is even though I created an amazing piece of work, and though I was fulfilled and joyful at the results, I also pushed the limits of my health. This is the yin and yang of passion: one can achieve great things but at times, it can come at a high cost.

This week discover what you are passionate about. Is it family, work, or maybe a hobby? Think about the way your passion can encourage your actions and how that affects you mentally and physically. Hold on to the passions you discover and the various ways they can improve your day, and life.

Journal:

1) How does passion play a role in your life? Do you have a passionate relationship, do you want to find the passion you remember from the past. How does it appear in your life?

2) Can you think of a time that passion was a negative emotion or had a negative result in your life? Write about it in depth so you can always understand its power.

3) Do you feel little or no passion in your life? Is there a need for you to look for what turns you on and creates the energy to move forward with energy? Write what you think will help to create this in your life.

Books:

The Agony and the Ecstasy: A Novel of Michelangelo written **by Irving Stone**

"Stone has painted the portrait of a supreme craftsman who was also one of the most versatile artists of all time." –This text refers to the Paperback edition.

In The Agony and the Ecstasy, the essential plot involving what many critics believe to be the ultimate of Michelangelo's painting focuses on the close but abrasive relationship between Pope Julius II and Michelangelo. Since this personal conflict resulted in the artist reluctantly painting the Sistine Chapel ceiling, by concentrating on this struggle, Stone is able to explore in detail the effect of a genius at work.

My Life in France by Julia Child

It was compiled by Julia Child and Alex Prud'homme, her husband's grandnephew, during the last eight months of her life, and completed and published by Prud'homme following her death in August 2004.

In her own words, it is a book about the things Julia loved most in her life: her husband, France (her "spiritual homeland"), and the "many pleasures of cooking and eating." It is a collection of linked autobiographical stories, mostly focused on the years between 1948 and 1954, recounting in detail the culinary experiences Julia and her husband, Paul Child, enjoyed while living in Paris, Marseilles, and Provence.

Julia Child had relentless drive and motivation. She did not let her passion for cooking die down, even after she failed the Cordon Bleu exam the first time. She practiced again, sharpened her technique, and passed when she attempted it the second time.

Films:

Pride and Prejudice directed by Joe Wright

Based on Jane Austen's 1813 novel of the same name. The film depicts five sisters from an English family of landed gentry as they deal with issues of marriage, morality and misconceptions. Keira Knightley stars in the lead role of Elizabeth Bennet, while Matthew Macfadyen plays her romantic interest Mr. Darcy. The story follows the main character Elizabeth Bennet as she deals with issues of manners, upbringing, morality, education, and marriage in the society of the landed gentry of early 19th-century England. Elizabeth is the second of five daughters of a country gentleman living near the fictional town of Meryton in Hertfordshire, near London.

Under the Tuscan Sun directed by Audrey Wells

From the studio that brought you Sweet Home Alabama comes the extraordinary romantic comedy starring Academy Award nominee Diane Lane (2002 Best Actress, Unfaithfull). Based on the #1 New York Times best-selling book Under theTuscan Sun follows San Francisco writer Frances Mayes (Lane) to Italy as a good friend offers her a special gift – 10 days in Tuscany. Once there, she is captivated by its beauty and warmth, and impulsively buys an aging, but very charming, villa. Fully embracing new friends and local color, she finds herself immersed in a life-changing adventure filled with enough unexpected surprises, laughter, friendship, and romance to restore her new home and her belief in second chances.

Midnight in Paris directed by Woody Allen starring Owen Wilson & Rachel McAdams

Gil Pender, a successful but creatively unfulfilled Hollywood screenwriter, and his fiancée, Inez, are in Paris, vacationing with Inez's wealthy, conservative parents. Gil is struggling to finish his first novel, centered on a man who works in a nostalgia shop, but Inez dismisses his ambition as a romantic daydream and encourages him to stick with the more lucrative screenwriting. While Gil is considering moving to Paris (which he notes, much to the dismay of his fiancée, is at its most beautiful in the rain), Inez is intent on living in Malibu. By chance, Inez's friend Paul, a pedantic pseudo-intellectual who speaks with great authority but questionable accuracy on the history and art of the city, joins them. Inez admires him, but Gil finds him insufferable.

The Aviator directed by Martin Scorsese starring Leonardo DiCaprio & Cate Blanchett

The Aviator is a 2004 American biographical drama film directed by Martin Scorsese, written by John Logan, produced by Graham King and Michael Mann and featuring an ensemble cast starring Leonardo DiCaprio, Cate Blanchett, Kate Beckinsale, Alan Alda, John C. Reilly and Alec Baldwin. It is the true story of aviation pioneer Howard Hughes, drawn largely upon numerous sources including a biography by Charles Higham. The film centers on Hughes' life from the late 1920s to 1947, during which time he became a successful film producer and an aviation magnate while simultaneously growing more unstable due to severe obsessive-compulsive disorder. The movie won five Oscars.

Quality

Quality

Quality is the excellence in and of everything

THE DICTIONARY DEFINITION
Quality is an adjective and noun

- of superior grade; choice wines; prime beef; prize carnations; quality paper; select peaches; the quality of mercy is not strained; each town has a quality all its own; the radical character of our demands; the timbre of her soprano was rich and lovely; the muffled tones of the broken bell summoned them to meet;

- of high social status; people of quality; a quality family; noun

- an essential and distinguishing attribute of something or someone;

- a degree or grade of excellence or worth; the quality of students has risen; an executive of low caliber;

- a characteristic property that defines the apparent individual nature of something;

- (Music) the distinctive property of a complex sound (a voice or noise or musical sound);

- High social status; a man of quality;

> It is the quality of our work which will please God and not the quantity.
>
> — Mahatma Gandhi

THE ISSUE OF QUALITY COMES UP FOR US WHEN WE THINK of the best, par excellence, our highest ideal and the level we want to achieve. When it comes to quality versus quantity, quality wins every time. Although more might be better when it comes to chocolate, not even that is better unless it is really excellent quality chocolate.

Quality is an expression of excellence. The best clothes, food, friends, or cars proves to the world that we demand the best, proves to ourselves that we deserve the best, and reflects an essence of us. As the quote from Gandhi states, "It is the quality of our work which will please God and not the quantity." This week, let's work from this statement.

When you begin the day do you think of doing the best you can do or doing the most you can do? I must admit that I am guilty of the latter. I am always doing too much and I know it often lessens the quality of my work, my relationships, and my time. I try to do it all, but unfortunately it is impossible to be in two places at the same time. One of my mentors, Natalie, an amazing woman of 92, once told me, "You cannot put your bottom in two seats at the same time, my dear!" She is correct and I do try to listen, but it is hard for me because I want it all!

There was an interesting article in the Atlantic Magazine entitled *Why Women Can't Still Have it All* by Anne Marie Slaughter – July/August 2012, you might enjoy the read. We need to decide on what we want to do with the thought of quality of life as the prerequisite of a balanced and fruitful life. The word quality is one that can be applied to our outer world as well as our inner one. We can all think of time that we have chosen more, rather than the best, in our lives.

This week focus on the importance of quality and its opposition to quantity. Endeavor to pursue all your tasks to the best of your ability and to bring the best you can into your life.

Journal:

1. Do you demand quality in your life? If you do, make a list of all the areas that you expect and receive it.

2. In what areas of your life do you see a great quality of life and in what areas do you see the lack of it? Do you feel your life is dull, ugly, mundane, or lacking in the qualities that would make your world a better place?

3. What is your most prized possession, person or experience? Write about the qualities that you love in them and define your quality of character.

Books:

Yesterday, I Cried : Celebrating the Lessons of Living and Loving by Iyanla Vanzant

Iyanla Vanzant has had an amazing and difficult life – one full of great challenges that have unmasked her wonderful gifts and led to the wisdom she has gained. In this simple book, she uses her own experiences to show how life's hardships can be re-visioned to become lessons that teach us as we grow, heal, and learn to love. Iyanla Vanzant is an example of how yesterday's tears become the seeds of today's hope, renewal, and strength.

Lean Forward into Your Life: Begin Each Day As If It Were on Purpose by Marry Anne Radmacher

Founder and owner of the Word Garden, Mary Anne Radmacher makes her art her life and her life an art. And in Lean Forward into Your Life she invites us to do the same. Or as she says, Lean Forward into Your Life is a commonplace book for leading an uncommon life. An uncommon life need not include fame and fortune. An uncommon life means living with intention, paying attention, celebrating, taking care of yourself, risking love. To live an uncommon life is to live large from the heart. Each section of Lean Forward into Your Life opens with a hand-lettered aphorism in the author's signature collage style. The essays, stories, and exercises that follow are designed to bring the reader into her or his own uncommon life.

The Invitation by Oriah Mountain Dreamer

This book brings to life the wisdom of her beloved *The Invitation,* the prose poem that has touched hearts everywhere with its fresh and spirited call to live life more passionately and honestly.
Speaking from the heart, she invites us to confront the varieties of human experience, from desire and commitment to sorrow and betrayal, and challenges us to open repeatedly to love and life. Unique, practical, and often surprising, *The Invitation* is an invaluable guide to living the ecstasy of everyday life, learning to recognize true beauty in ourselves and the world, and finding the sustenance our spirit longs for.

Films:

Gia directed by Michael Cristofer starring Angelina Jolie & Faye Dunaway

Gia Carangi (Angelina Jolie) is a Philadelphia native who moves to New York City to become a fashion model and immediately catches the attention of powerful agent Wilhelmina Cooper(Faye Dunaway). Gia's attitude and beauty help her rise quickly to the forefront of the modeling industry, but her persistent loneliness after the death of Wilhelmina drives her to experiment with mood-altering drugs like cocaine. She becomes entangled in a passionate affair with Linda (Elizabeth Mitchell), a make-up artist. Failed attempts at reconciliation with Linda and with her mother, Kathleen (Mercedes Ruehl), drive Gia to begin abusing heroin. Although she is eventually able to break her drug habit after much effort, she has already contracted HIV from a needle containing infected blood and dies from complications from AIDS in 1986 at the age of 26.

A Wonderful Life produced and directed by Frank Capra, with James Stewart

The film was based on the short story "The Greatest Gift", written by Philip Van Doren Stern in 1939, and privately published by the author in 1945. The film is considered one of the most inspirational and best loved movies in American cinema.

In Bedford Falls, New York on Christmas Eve, George Bailey (James Stewart) is deeply troubled. Prayers for his well being from friends and family reach Heaven. Clarence Odbody (Henry Travers), Angel Second Class, is assigned to save George and earn his wings. Franklin and Joseph, the head angels, review George's life with Clarence. At the age of 12, George (Bobby Anderson) saved his younger brother Harry (George Nokes), who had fallen through the ice on a frozen pond, though George lost the hearing in his left ear in this effort. Later, working in the local pharmacy, George luckily noticed that druggist Mr. Gower (H. B. Warner), despondent over his son's death, had mistakenly filled a child's prescription with poison and saved the poor man from irrevocably ruining his own life by inadvertently killing the child.

Response

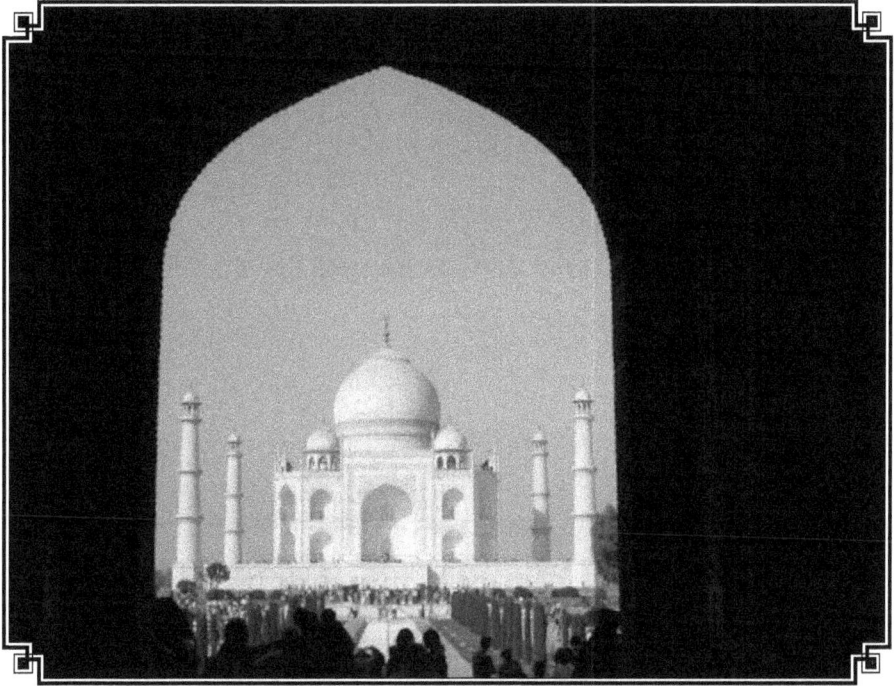

Response

Response is the choice you make subsequent to an event

THE DICTIONARY DEFINITION
Response is a noun

- a result; this situation developed in response to events in Africa; a bad reaction to the medicine; his responses have slowed with age; I waited several days for his answer; he wrote replies to several of his critics;

- a bodily process occurring due to the effect of some foregoing stimulus or agent;

- a statement (either spoken or written) that is made in reply to a question or request or criticism or accusation;

- the manner in which something is greeted; she did not expect the cold reception she received from her superiors;

- a phrase recited or sung by the congregation following a versicle by the priest or minister

- the speech act of continuing a conversational exchange; he growled his reply;

"When you have a challenge and the response is equal
to the challenge, that's called "success." But once you
have a new challenge, the old, once-successful response no
longer works. That's why it is called a "failure."

— Stephen R. Covey

WHEN I ATTENDED JACK CANFIELD'S SEVEN-DAY WORKSHOP in Santa Barbara I was given a number of useful techniques to becoming a better teacher. One of the most vivid lessons was E + R = O. The Event plus the Response equals the Outcome. I hold this as one of my truths: it is not the events in our lives, but our response to these events, that have the power to shift our reality.

Think about it, do you respond to a small fender bender with a calm acceptance, anger, or fear? Like attitude your response is a choice. Watch yourself and those around you for responses to events and you will be amazed by the different reactions. These responses can reveal a lot about an individual through their behavior and thoughts. I have watched my responses many times and have learned a lot about who I am and who I want to be. Think back to a situation that had a bad outcome. Reenact it in your mind but alter your response, and imagine what the outcome might have been. By doing so, you will know what to do the next time you experience a similar situation and opt for a different, possibly better, outcome.

I was trying to think of one of the times I had a positive response to a difficult event, and the one that came to mind was a little fender bender I had while parking my new car on a hill that was slick from recent rainfall. I was frustrated by the difficulty of finding a parking spot because there were so many cars on the street. When I finally found a spot and put my car into reverse, it slid into a brand new Audi! I was upset for a moment, and then I realized that it was probably a person who was also attending the special birthday party for my dear friend Beth's eight year-old quadruplets!

This was an important day and I decided not to let a small bump on two cars ruin it, so I went to the party and I enjoyed the birthday celebration. When the entertainment was over, I told my friend I bumped into another car on the street. Before I could finish the woman next to her said, "I hope it wasn't my new Audi!" I had to admit it was her car, and I offered to take care of the damage and give her my insurance information. I apologized profusely but her reply was the best. She looked at me and with loving kind eyes and said, "I have always wanted to know you better and have respected your work since you were with Women's Economic Ventures, so don't worry it will be fine. Now we can talk on the phone and get to know each other better." It was an amazing response to an unfortunate circumstance and it created a new friendship and an experience that could have been awful turned out to be just fine.

This week is a time for contemplation about your own experiences. Look back on the different ways you observe situations and your responses to them. Consider the possibility of different outcomes to some situations in your life and how they could have resulted. As you uncover these possibilities you can discover new parts of who you are and how you can become the person you want to be.

Journal:

1) What do you remember an event that was difficult but turned out well because of the choice that you made in your response?

2) Do you remember and event that you created a bad outcome because of your response and if you could change it what would you have done differently.

3) Take this week to look at all the events and response you have to those events and make a list. At the end of the week look at the list and see where you could have improved the response and where your response was the perfect one for that particular event.

Books:

The Choice by Eliyahu M. Goldratt

The book explains his way of thinking about reality and the consequences of thinking clearly. The book is structured as a dialogue between the author and his daughter Efrat, where he attempts to explain clearly the way he thinks, and the obstacles that prevent people from thinking in the same fashion. Interspersed between the dialogues are short cases that demonstrate or further explore the points raised in the discussion. The content of this book might be seen as explaining the basic principles upon which are based the TOC Thinking Processes.

Disaster Response and Recovery by David A. McEntire

Providing readers with a well-rounded understanding of disaster responses, this book first explores the various types of disasters that may occur. It then uncovers the myriad of actors that are involved in emergency management as well as the diverse theoretical frameworks from which post-disaster activities may be approached. Readers will gain a better understanding of the typical challenges to be expected during response efforts as well as the tools and techniques that will enhance the ability to protect lives, reduce property damage and minimize disruption.

Films:

The Brotherhood directed by David DeCoteau starring Barry Levy & Matthew Jason Walsh

Adam Buckley finds himself in the middle of a convenience store robbery during his last night as a pledge for a college fraternity. When the initiation ritual goes horribly wrong, and every move proves disastrous, Adam is forced to confront a new challenge all together, and he has to take a stand. *Written by Anonymous*

The Help - Directed by Tate Taylor. Starring Emma Stone, Viola Davis.

Set in Jackson, Mississippi, 1962: aspiring writer Eugenia "Skeeter" an aspiring author during the civil rights movement of the 1960s decides to write a book detailing the African-American maids' point of view on the white families for which they work, and the hardships they go through on a daily basis.

Spirit

Spirit

Spirit is in everything. It is the secular version of God.

THE DICTIONARY DEFINITION
Spirit is both a noun and a verb

- the vital principle or animating force within living things the feel of the city excited him; a clergyman improved the tone of the meeting; it had the smell of treason; his emotional state depended on her opinion; he was in good spirits; his spirit rose;

- the general atmosphere of a place or situation and the effect that it has on people;

- a fundamental emotional and activating principle determining one's character

- any incorporeal supernatural being that can become visible (or audible) to human beings

- the state of a person's emotions (especially with regard to pleasure or dejection);

- the intended meaning of a communication

- animation and energy in action or expression; it was a heavy play and the actors tried in vain to give life to it;

- an inclination or tendency of a certain kind; he had a change of heart; verb

- infuse with spirit; The company spirited him up;

You ask why I make my home in the mountain forest, and I
smile, and am silent, and even my soul remains quiet;
it lives in another world which no one owns.
The peach trees blossom, The water flows...

— Li Po

Spirit lives in all of us. It is the energy that fuels our cells to form and grow. Today the word spirit is incorporated in our vocabulary as never before: it is a reference to our souls or to a higher power. I often wonder if this is the result of a decrease in church attendance and an increase in alternative ways to make our lives sacred. We do not need a person, place, or deity to connect with spirit, or any other higher power we may believe in. The only prerequisite to such a connection is a belief in a higher power, that it lives forever, and exists as our guide through life.

This understanding can be difficult for some and comforting for others. Why does Spirit hold such interest for us? Is it our need to connect, to be heard, or have a guide? I believe Spirit functions for all this and more. Spirit is the energy that fuels my soul and keeps me healthy. It sparks my creativity, answers my prayers, and connects me to all things. In Spirit I feel that all is possible and that we are not alone

As I try to imagine when I felt spirit in my life, the story of a woman named Susan comes to mind. When I was teaching one of the first classes at Women's Economic Ventures in the early 1990s, I had a student come up to me after a class and ask if I knew an Alan Weisbart. I said, "Yes, he is my stepson." Susan smiled and said, "You must be the good stepmom!" With that she began to tell me about her relationship with Alan when he was in high school years before. She was his counselor through difficult times during his transition to live with his father and me. She supported him when he needed her most, and when he needed understanding.

I was amazed by this relation, and felt the hairs on my neck rise as she told me her story. I felt like a spirit was speaking through her about my beloved stepson, transcending her connection from him to me. It was a moment of clarity and love. This woman touched my soul through spirit. Susan remains a dear friend and we see each other often. Our friendship is magical and very important to me. I am grateful each day for the gift of spirit and what it gives me.

This week is the time for you to look at your beliefs in God, spirit, and the energy of light. Discover how your beliefs allow you to feel connected to the people and environment around you.

Appreciate the ways in which you connect and learn through Spirit, and what you gain through these connections.

Journal:

1) This may be a difficult week for you if you don't believe in God, Spirit or a religion. So if you do not, please work on the idea that every atom is animated and think on where that comes from and how it works.

2) Read, meditate, and pray about the meaning of Spirit in your life. Enjoy the process; become connected with your spirit and the universal one.

3) In many religions it is believed that your sacred space is the manifestation of holy. Go to or create a scared space to think and ponder what spirit means to you.

Books:

Man's Quest for God by Abraham Heschel

Dr Abraham Joshua Heschel, professor of Ethics and Mysticism at the Jewish Theological Seminary in New York, was one of the outstanding philosophers and theologians of our time. Internationally acclaimed author, scholar, activist and theologian, Dr Heschels classic, "Mans Quest for God", originally published in 1954, continues to be a significant contribution to contemporary Jewish literature. In his poetic and inspiring style, Heschel offers insights that speak deeply to the essence of prayer.

Rumi: a spiritual biography

Presents an intriguing portrait of the thirteenth-century Sufi mystic, describing his youth in Afghanistan and Turkey, beliefs, spirituality, poetry, and political influence, in a study that also examines his impact on twentieth-century mysticism and literature.

Toward a True Kinship of Faiths by His Holiness the Dalai Lama

In the past, religious conflict has fueled strife among people the world over. Although the consequences have been significant and tragic, these conflicts did not threaten the very survival of humankind. With the advent of globalization, the increase in terrorism, and the creation of weapons of mass destruction, this is no longer the case. In this book, the Dalai Lama addresses this concern. He wishes to show an alternative path toward peaceful coexistence. He shows how globalization can bring people together to foster a deeper understanding and appreciation by way of their rich spiritual traditions and their shared human experience.

Autobiography of a Yogi by Paramahansa Yogananda

Autobiography of a Yogi introduces the reader to the life of Paramahansa Yogananda and his encounters with spiritual figures of both the East and West. The book begins with his childhood family life, to finding his guru, to becoming a monk and establishing his teachings of Kriya Yoga meditation. The book continues in 1920 when Yogananda accepts an invitation to speak in a religious congress in Boston, Massachusetts, USA. He then travels across America lecturing and establishing his teachings in Los Angeles, California. In 1935 he returns to India for a yearlong visit. When he returns to America, he continues to establish his teachings, including writing this book. The book is an introduction to the methods of attaining God-realization and to the spiritual thought of the East, which had only been available to a few in 1946. The author claims that the writing of the book was prophesied long ago by the nineteenth-century master Lahiri Mahasaya.

Films:

What the Bleep Do We Know!? Directed by William Arntz, Betsy Chasse and Mark Vicenic

A 2004 film that combines documentary-style interviews, computer-animated graphics, and a narrative that posits a spiritual connection between quantum physics and consciousness. The plot follows the story of a photographer as she encounters emotional and existential obstacles in her life and begins to consider the idea that individual and group consciousness can influence the material world. Her experiences are offered by the filmmakers to illustrate the movie's thesis about quantum physics and consciousness.

The Shawshank Redemption written and directed by Frank Darabont and starring Tim Robbins and Morgan Freeman.

Adapted from the Stephen King novella Rita Hayworth and Shawshank Redemption, the film tells the story of Andy Dufresne, a banker who spends nearly two decades in Shawshank State Prison for the murder of his wife and her lover despite his claims of innocence. During his time at the prison, he befriends a fellow inmate, Ellis Boyd "Red" Redding, and finds himself protected by the guards after the warden begins using him in his money laundering operation.

Finding Neverland directed by Marc Forster starring Johnny Depp and Kate Winslet

This is a 2004 semi-biographical film about playwright J. M. Barrie and his relationship with a family who in following the dismal reception of his latest play, *Little Mary*, Barrie meets the widowed Sylvia and her four young sons in Kensington Gardens, and a strong friendship develops between them. He proves to be a great playmate and surrogate father figure for the boys, and their imaginative antics give him ideas which he incorporates into a play about boys who do not want to grow up, especially one named after troubled young Peter Llewelyn Davies. His wife Mary, who eventually divorces him, and Sylvia's mother Emma du Maurier, object to the amount of time Barrie spends with the Llewelyn Davies family. Emma also seeks to control her daughter and grandsons, especially as Sylvia becomes increasingly weak from an unidentified illness.

Talent

Talent

THE AUTHOR'S MEANING

Talent is the birthright given to us as currency in our lives.

THE DICTIONARY DEFINITION

Talent is a noun

- natural qualities or talents
- a person who possesses unusual innate ability in some field or activity

> Everyone has talent. What is rare is the courage to follow the talent to the dark place where it leads.
>
> — Erica Jong

MANY PEOPLE BELIEVE THEY HOLD NO TALENT, WHICH I find to be sad and untrue. I believe we are all given talents when we are born; they are gifts we are entrusted with to create the world. Everyone is here to make a mark on the world and our talents are the passports.

Talents can be great and seen by others, or they can be quiet and personal. It really does not matter how these talents appear as long as they do. The talents you hold can reveal your true identity and reflect inner aspirations. If your talents are art, writing, sewing, or cooking, do them for the pure joy of doing them because some talents are disguised as our hobbies. Those who have talents in areas of music, dance, mathematics and speaking are often more noticed than others, but that is not what I am calling for in this chapter. The significance of talent is not in its perceptibility.

It is important to experience the energy your talents give you. Some talents are not "doing" anything. Maybe your talent is listening, inspiring others, healing, or thinking. All these types of activities are also talents in a form that does not require physical action. It is your job to honor whatever talents you have. Help them grow and give thanks for them: your talent makes you unique.

My story this week is of the talent I saw emerge from my mother at the age of sixty-four. My mom was a widow since her late 30's and never had time to find a talent that did not include caring for her family, or making a living. At sixty-four she retired from her job and attended an art class. She never had any experience with art prior to the class because she felt she never had the time. It is a shame she felt that way because once she began the work she loved it. Her talent was evident in her work and the prizes she has won. Now at the age of ninety-two, she still dabbles in painting and drawing because it gives her joy. It was a blessing to finally find her hidden gift. It is never too late to find yours.

This week discover your hidden talents. Rekindle your passion for your hobbies and work to excel in them. Your talents can change your day, and sometimes even your life. Pursuing our talents can enrich our lives and bring us to a better place of fulfillment. Take the time to infuse the positivity of your talents in your life and cherish the experience of engaging in them.

Journal:

1) Where do your talents lie? Can you make a list of those you know you possess and those you would like to cultivate?

2) What talents can you see in others around you? Can you help them to see them and to use them?

3) Do you believe that talents are a birthright or do you create them in yourself? Can you learn to play music, do art, and inspire others just by working at it? If so, what have you done to build a talent in you?

Books:

The Talent Code by Daniel Coyle

What is the secret of talent? How do we unlock it? In this ground-breaking work, journalist and New York Times bestselling author Daniel Coyle provides parents, teachers, coaches, businesspeople—and everyone else—with tools they can use to maximize potential in themselves and others. Whether you're coaching soccer or teaching a child to play the piano, writing a novel or trying to improve your golf swing, this revolutionary book shows you how to grow talent by tapping into a newly discovered brain mechanism. Drawing on cutting-edge neurology and firsthand research gathered on journeys to nine of the world's talent hotbeds—from the baseball fields of the Caribbean to a classical-music academy in upstate New York—Coyle identifies the three key elements that will allow you to develop your gifts and optimize your performance in sports, art, music, math, or just about anything.

Diane Arbus: A Biography by Patricia Bosworth

Diane Arbus's unsettling photographs of dwarves and twins, trans-vestites and giants, both polarized and inspired, and her work had already become legendary when she committed suicide in 1971. This groundbreaking biography examines the private life behind Arbus's controversial art. The book deals with Arbus's pampered Manhattan childhood, her passionate marriage to Allan Arbus, their work together as fashion photographers, the emotional upheaval surrounding the end of their marriage, and the radical, liberating, and ultimately tragic turn Arbus's art took during the 1960s when she was so richly productive.

Films:

August Rush directed by Kirsten Sheridan starring Kerrie Russell & William Sadler

This movie is about an orphan whose parents were both exceptionally talented musicians. The father was in a band; the mother was a renowned classical instrumentalist who performed at Julliard. His grandfather gave up the young boy, whose name is August, for adoption because he was born out of wedlock. August has no evidence that his parents are alive, but by following his talent (the ability to hear music and harmony from various city sounds), he is eventually reunited with them. This is one of my all-time favorite movies.

Bagdad Café directed by Percy Adlon starring Marianne Sägebrecht, CCH Pounder and Jack Palance

The film is a comedy set in a remote truck-stop café and motel in the Mojave Desert. It centers around two women who have recently separated from their husbands, and the blossoming friendship, which ensues. The film begins with a fight between German tourist Jasmin Münchgstettner (Sägebrecht) from Rosenheim and her husband whilst they are driving across the desert. She storms out of the car and happens upon the truck stop run by the tough-as-nails and short tempered Brenda (Pounder), whose own husband, after an argument out front, is soon to leave as well. Jasmin takes a room at the adjacent motel. Initially suspicious of the foreigner, Brenda eventually befriends Jasmin and allows her to work at the café. The café is visited by an assortment of colorful characters, including a strange ex-Hollywood set-painter (Palance) and a glamorous tattoo artist (Kaufmann). The film has a melodious backdrop in the form of J. S. Bach preludes played on piano by Brenda's son (Darron Flagg). With an ability to quietly empathize with everyone she meets at the café, helped by a passion for cleaning and performing magic tricks, Jasmin gradually transforms the café and all the people in it.

Unconditional

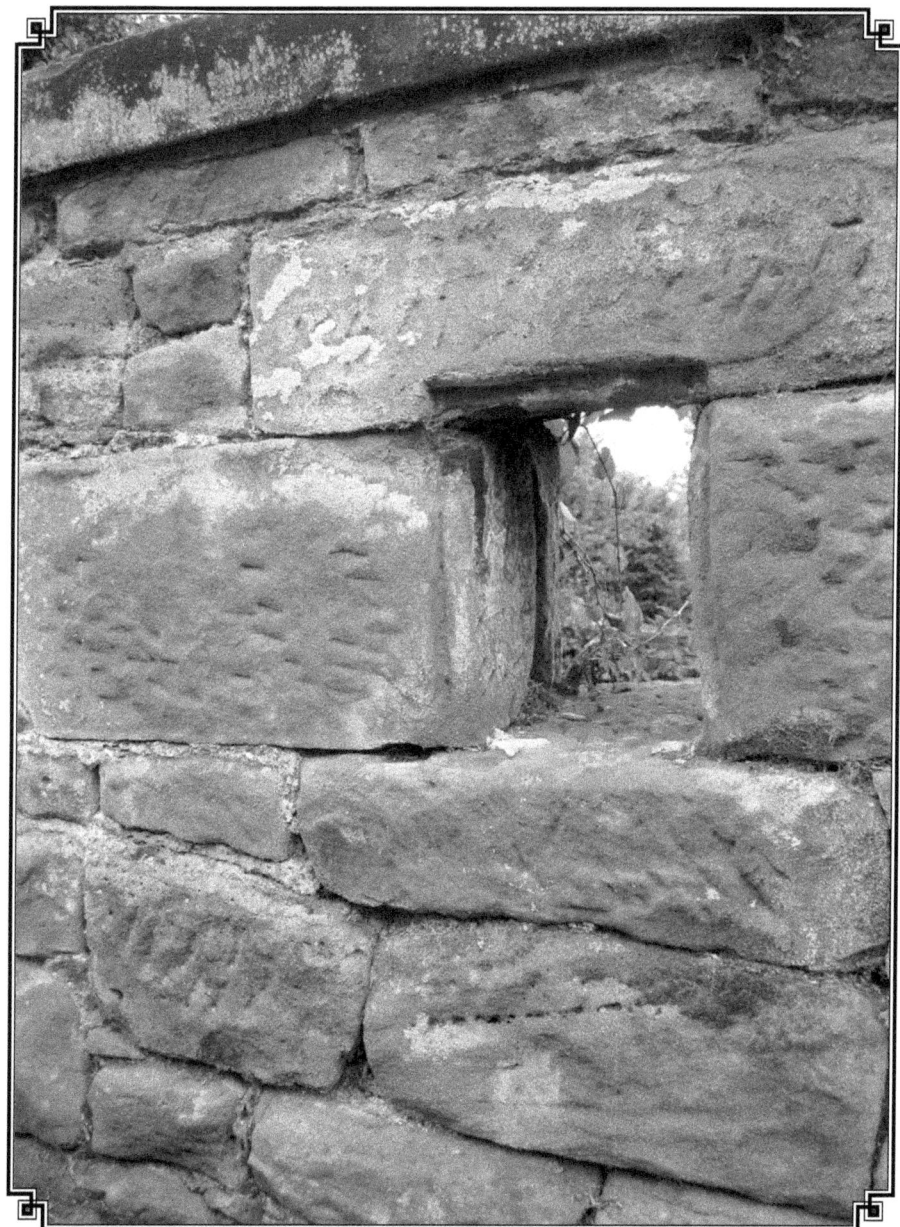

Unconditional

Unconditional is the consciousness to reject judgments.

THE DICTIONARY DEFINITION
Unconditional is an adjective

- not conditional; unconditional surrender;

- not modified or restricted by reservations; a categorical denial; a flat refusal;

- not contingent; not determined or influenced by someone or something else.

> Love is a force that connects us to every strand of the universe, an unconditional state that characterizes human nature, a form of knowledge that is always there for us if only we can open ourselves to it.
>
> — Emily Hilburn Sell

WE ARE ALL JUDGMENTAL AND CONDITIONAL IN OUR relationships, and to be unconditional takes great determination. To be a person with no judgment is impossible because in some cases you must be able to assess ideas, people, and situations. We need to be able to make judgments about a purpose, intention, or relationship that affects our lives. Good judgment is as important to survival as unconditional love. The purpose of this chapter is to analyze your ability to have no conditions, no expectations and live a more abundant and loving life.

When a child is born we must have unconditional love because the infant cannot fulfill any of its needs. They can only eat, sleep, and make sounds. As humans grow conditions are placed on them to achieve, to behave, to be what the parent wants them to be. This is why the act of being unconditional is a higher consciousness. To love unconditionally is to have no other values placed on the person other than acceptance and the sheer joy of love.

The question is how to put aside all judgment and simply love. I believe we can do this because it gives us such joy and freedom to do so. Though I often find this difficult I pursue it with fervor because I know when I achieve this state I have less pain and suffering. Let me explain. When one has exceptions about a person, event or outcome we suffer because most of the time it doesn't work the way we want it to work. In Buddhism it is said that much suffering is caused by expectations. Thus, if you have no conditions then you have no expectations, meaning you have no suffering.

Lets go back to that newborn I spoke of before. She grows to be a woman but instead of using her talents of caring for others and becoming a nurse, she becomes a drug dealer. Is she still loved? Well, it might be difficult to love her if it is not unconditional, but if she is seen as a loving person who deserves love no matter what then the answer is yes! Unconditional is a word that has many issues attached to it. So this week lets look into our hearts and souls and see whether you can identify your unconditional center.

Journal:

1) Look into your heart and mind where you are able to find your pure joy and the place where conditions and judgments are suspended. Write about them and how you feel when you act in this way.

2) When have you felt that you were unconditionally loved, accepted, or understood? Have you ever had this experience? If not who would you like to give it to and who would you like to receive it from?

3) Do you know of any times that this has occurred in the world. When a situation was changed for the better because conditions and judgments were suspended.

Books:

America is in the Heart by Carlos Bulosan

This autobiography is about an immigrant Filipino farm worker. He masters the art of writing an autobiography by reaching that Asian American point of view and has been regarded as "the premier text of the delicate balance that makes up a neutral tone. He is neither overly aggressive nor passive in his book, but he conveys his experiences beautifully in a way that illuminates his unconditional hope for a better day, a better America. The novel was one of the earliest published books that presented the experiences of the immigrant and working class based on a Filipino-American experience. "In his introduction, journalist Carey McWilliams, who wrote a 1939 study about migrant farm labor in California (*Factories in the Field*), described *America Is in the Heart* as a "social classic" that reflected on the experiences of Filipino immigrants in America who were searching for the "promises of a better life"

The Four Loves by C. S. Lewis

This book explores the nature of love from a Christian perspective through thought experiments. The content of the examination is prefaced by Lewis' admission that he initially mistook St. John's words "God is Love" as a simple beginning point to address the topic. But further meditation revealed two different kinds of love: "need-love" (such as the love of a child for its mother) as distinguished from "gift-love" (epitomized by God's love for humanity). Lewis happened upon the insight that the natures of even these basic categorizations of love are more complicated than they seem at first. As a result of this, he formulates the foundation of his topic by exploring the nature of pleasure, and then divides love into four categories ("the highest does not stand without the lowest"), based in part on the four Greek words for love: affection, friendship, eros, and charity. Lewis states that just as Lucifer—a former archangel—perverted himself by pride and fell into depravity, so too can love—commonly held to be the arch-emotion—become corrupt by presuming itself to be what it is not.

Films:

Ladder 49 directed by Jay Russell with Joaquin Phoenix and John Travolta

This is a movie about a wife's unconditional love and support for her husband, even when his career threatened the foundation of their family. A 2004 film about the heroics of a Baltimore fireman Jack Morrison, who is trapped inside a warehouse fire and his recollection of the events that got him to that point. Back at the grain building fire, Jack's fellow firefighters become extremely determined to rescue him and Jack does his best to reach the possible safe area that Mike told him about. However, upon reaching that room he sees that the only exit is cut off by raging flames and Jack realizes that his situation is hopeless. He radios Mike to pull his men back, so no one else will be hurt while trying to rescue him. Mike reluctantly agrees and Jack accepts his fate to die in the fire, devastating Mike. At Jack's funeral, Mike delivers an emotional <u>eulogy</u>, which ends with a standing ovation, in celebration of Jack's life, from friends and family in attendance.

Man on Fire directed by Tony Scott with Denzel Washington, Christopher Walken & Dakota Fanning

This movie is about unconditional dedication and determination of a bodyguard (Denzel Washington) to protecting a young girl. No measure is too far for him when an organized crime gang in Mexico abducts her and he has to return her to safety.

Because of the extremely high rate of kidnappings in Mexico City for ransom money, businessman Samuel Ramos (Marc Anthony) hires former Marine Force Recon officer and CIA operative John Creasy (Denzel Washington) to guard his nine year-old daughter "Pita" (Dakota Fanning). At first Creasy distances himself socially from Pita, but the two develop a friendship. After a piano lesson, Pita is abducted in public and Creasy is shot multiple times. The Ramos' agree to deliver a dead drop ransom of US$10 million per the instructions of "The Voice" (Roberto Sosa), the mastermind of the kidnapping ring. Members of a Mexican crime syndicate, however, ambush the drop, and the money is stolen, resulting in The Voice notifying the Ramoses that Pita will not be returned. Upon hearing the news, Creasy leaves the hospital before fully recovering from his wounds and vows to Pita's mother Lisa (Radha Mitchell) that he will kill everyone involved in her abduction.

Vision

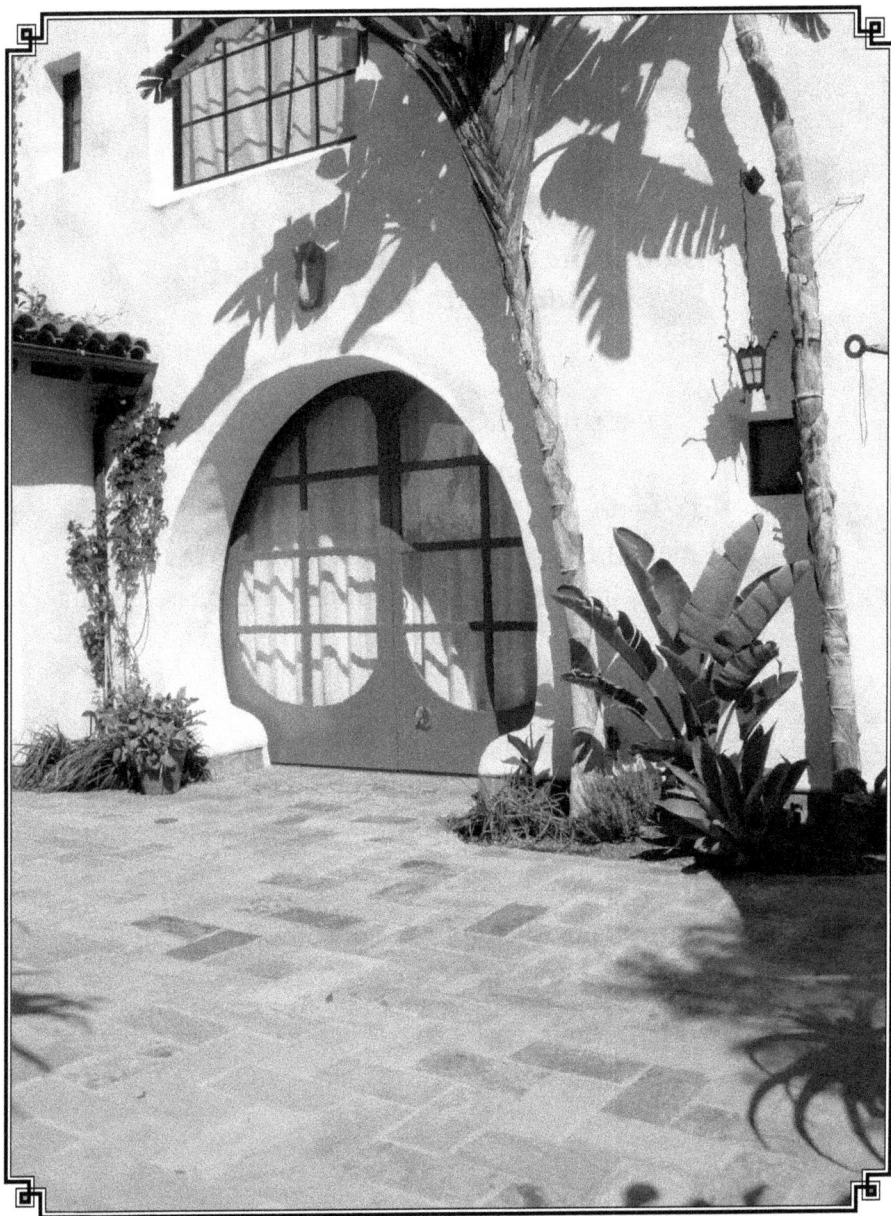

Vision

Vision is the ability to see beyond the mundane into the future.

THE DICTIONARY DEFINITION

Vision is a noun

- a vivid mental image; he had a vision of his own death; popular imagination created a world of demons; imagination reveals what the world could be; he had a vision of the Virgin Mary;

- the ability to see; the faculty of vision

- the perceptual experience of seeing; the runners emerged from the trees into his clear vision; he had a visual sensation of intense light;

- the formation of a mental image of something that is not perceived as real and is not present to the senses;

- a religious or mystical experience of a supernatural appearance;

Far away there in the sunshine are my highest aspirations.
I may not reach them, but I can look up and see their beauty,
believe in them, and try to follow where they lead.

— Louisa May Alcott

I OFTEN FEEL AWE WHEN I HAVE THE VISION I NEED TO surpass the mundane view of life. It is a gift given to those who are willing to live with faith: faith in the future and the unknown. Vision is a dream beyond our imaginings and an ability to shift our attention from this moment to the next. It is the one thing that moves humanity from caves to penthouses, and beyond to the heavens. When Jules Vern wrote *Ten Thousand Leagues Under the Sea*, did he know that one-day submarines would be passé? Did the Wright brothers know that we would fly into space when they created the Kitty Hawk? Probably not. The visionaries are the seeds to the future, but these huge world-changing acts are not the only types of visions.

My vision was to have one person at a time work on the *Portals of Life* and go deep inside themselves to manifest a better life, community, and world. Now here you are reading this, and it is time for you to write about your visions. With faith in the future you can create a new world for tomorrow. It is a blessing to share the visions we see, and watch them manifest when others see them and help to make them real.

My story for this week is about a vision I had when I was carving a piece of stone. I literally saw a face in the stone when it was lying on the ground in the stone yard. When I finally got it to my studio and on the carving bench, it only took me ten hours to cut away the extra stone and show the beauty of "Woman," a piece I sold shortly after for a hefty sum of money. The time from my vision to its manifestation was not long, but the result was powerful and exciting. Vision is a gift for our futures and for our lives.

This week expand your ability to go above and beyond. Take a chance on the unknown and embrace the power to be a force of change or discovery. If you have a vision, consider the ways you can empower yourself to make it real. Digging into our imaginations to bring our ideas to life can enrich our lives and be very liberating for our minds.

Journal:

1) Write about the ideas and moments that you have felt like you see beyond your mundane life into a bigger world. If you have not had this experience in your life write about what you want to see in your future

2) When imagining a possible future event do you visualize it? If so do write this down? If you have never visualized please listen to my visualization on www.theportalsoflife.com and get a feeling for visioning.

3) What would be the best way for you to manifest a vision, what would you need to do, who would you need to involve? Write about what it would take for you to do this. Check out a vision board.

Books:

Living the Life of Your Dreams by Marilyn Tam

The Secrets of Turning Your Dreams into Reality" she reveals the secrets, principles, tools and strategies she and other experts learned and used to achieve a balanced, healthy and joyful life. People want contentment, love and happiness from meaningful work, personal relationships, healthy mind and body, a spiritual core and a reason for living. This book is filled with stories, tips and insights on how anyone can live the life they've dreamed of living - a happy, healthy, successful and dynamically balanced life.

The Vision Board: The Secret to an Extraordinary Life by Joyce Schwarz

Find out who you are and achieve what you most want in life with *The Vision Board*. Through the exercises and inspirational success stories included in this book, you can clarify your true vision and create a personal vision board. Learn the five secrets to living the life of your dreams.

Life Visioning: A Transformative Process for Activating Your Unique Gifts and Highest Potential by Michael Bernard Beckwith

Why have you been given this singular treasure that is your life and how will you use it? What is the purpose for the unique blend of gifts, skills, experiences, and perspectives that you alone possess? To support you in answering these questions and living in sync with your inner calling, Michael Bernard Beckwith presents *Life Visioning*-an essential companion for anyone seeking to accelerate their spiritual evolution. Michael Beckwith created the Life Vision- ing Process to be a transformational technology for applying deep inquiry and spiritual practice to enable the growth, development, and enfoldment of your soul. With *Life Visioning,* he details the process in its entirety, with invaluable insights and meditations to help you each step of the way.

Films:

The Secret directed by Sean Byrne & Drew Heriot

The Secret, described as a self-help film, uses a documentary format to present the Law of Attraction. As described in the film, the "Law of Attraction" principle posits that feelings and thoughts can attract events, feelings, and experiences, from the workings of the cosmos to interactions among individuals in their physical, emotional, and professional affairs. The film also suggests that there has been a strong tendency by those in positions of power to keep this central principle hidden from the public.

The Diary of Anne Frank directed by George Stevens starring Millie Perkins, Joseph Schildkraut & Shelley Winters

Harrowing story of a young Jewish girl who, with her family and their friends is forced into hiding in an attic in Nazi-occupied Amsterdam. *The Diary of Anne Frank* is a 1959 film based on the Pulitzer Prize winning play of the same name, which was based on the diary of Anne Frank. It won three Academy Awards. It is the first film version of both the play and the original story, and features three members of the original Broadway cast. The movie was based on the personal diary of Anne Frank, a Jewish girl who lived in a hiding place with her family during World War II. All her writings to her diary were addressed as 'Dear Kitty'. The diary was published after the end of the war by her father Otto Frank by this time all his other family members were killed by the Nazis.

Rudy: directed by David Anspaugh starring Sean Astin, Jon Fayreau & Ned Beatty

Daniel Eugene "Rudy" Ruettiger grows up in Joliet, Illinois dreaming of playing college football at the University of Notre Dame While achieving some success with his local high school team (Joliet Catholic), he lacks the grades and money to attend Notre Dame (which is not only a big football power, but also very academically prestigious), not to mention talent and physical size. During his final semester of transfer eligibility, Rudy is admitted to Notre Dame. He rushes home to tell his family. At the steel mill, his father announces it over the loudspeaker, "Hey, you guys, my son's going to Notre Dame!"

Devine finally lets Rudy enter the field with the defensive team on the final kickoff. He stays in for the final play of the game, sacks the Georgia Tech quarterback, and is carried off on the shoulders of his teammates.

Visions of a Universal Humanity or Humanity Ascending by Barbara Marx Hubbard

In Visions, futurist Barbara Marx Hubbard brings together some of the finest minds of our time, presenting us with positive, future scenarios for humanity based on the latest scientific, social and spiritual realities.

Wisdom

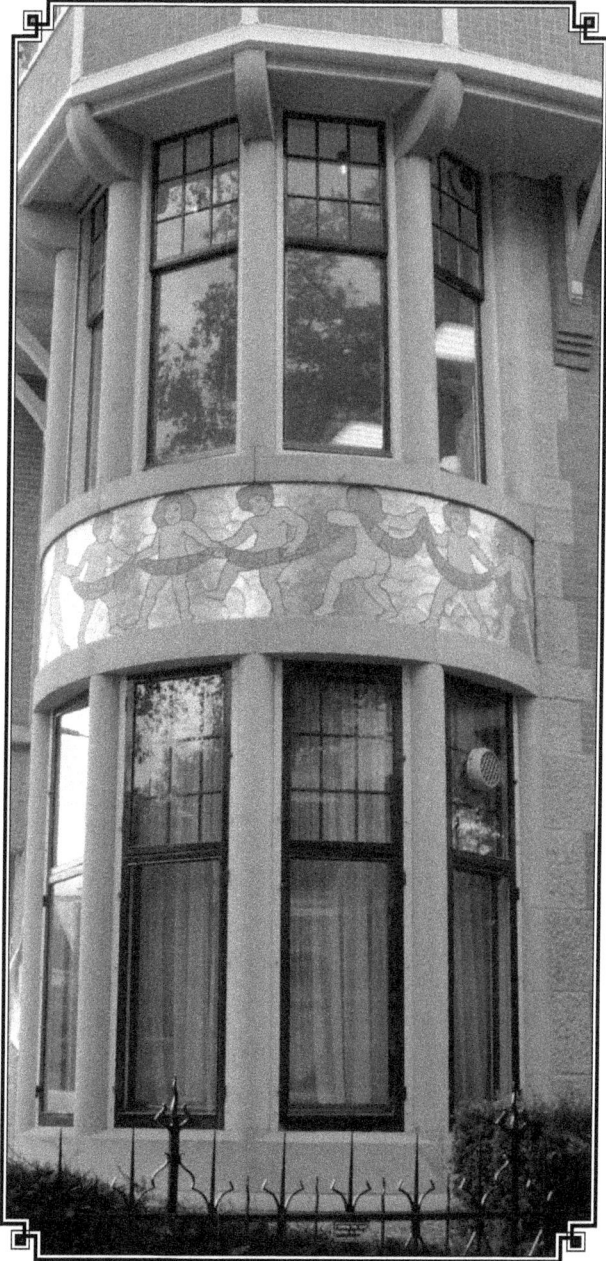

Wisdom

Wisdom is knowledge combined with compassion and love

THE DICTIONARY DEFINITION
Wisdom is a noun

- accumulated knowledge or erudition or enlightenment

- the trait of utilizing knowledge and experience with common sense and insight

- ability to apply knowledge or experience or understanding or common sense and insight

- the quality of being prudent and sensible

- an Apocryphal book consisting mainly of a meditation on wisdom; although ascribed to Solomon it was probably written in the first century BC

> "God, grant me the serenity to accept the things I cannot change, the courage to change the things I can, and the wisdom to know the difference.
>
> — Reinhold Niebuhr

WISDOM IS THE CULMINATION OF LOVE AND KNOWLEDGE, and it comes across all ages. It can be apparent in a homeless man, a leader, and is not limited to any gender, race, or financial circumstance. Wisdom is a blessing but to be wise one must always be a student and open to information. We must also be willing to learn through focus and humility, which will allow the virtue of knowledge to develop.

An illness early in my life taught me to focus and be humble, and through the experience I was enlightened to the greatest wisdom of my life: acceptance and release. If these two actions are done in order life can be a breeze, but like many things, it is easier said than done. Throughout the ages, wise ones have taught of God, the meaning of life, and a number of insightful messages, bringing to mind different knowledgeable subjects. I believe wisdom is in us all. It is understood when we take the time to listen to others and to our inner voices. We need to continually search for knowledge and couple it with love and compassion to attain a level of wisdom.

The wisest person in my life is my mother, and the teaching that always stuck in my head is the knowledge that life is a gift. It is given to us and we must live it to our fullest capabilities. My mother always told me to "make a decision and move forward!" Her wisdom is to move forward no matter what happens in your life. When my mother was thirty-eight years old she became a widow and she didn't know which way to turn. She was troubled with the decision to move her children with her from the United States to her native country, England. She asked one of her old friends for advice and was told something that changed the course of her life. My mother's friend told her that you can never know the out come of a decision, but you must make it and stand by the decision to move forward. This to me is great advice and true wisdom. The hardships and obstacles in our lives are often made worse by our inability to move on or make a decision. Wisdom helps to motivate us to live better lives, and provide us the tools to thrive in many circumstances.

This week reflect on the most important wisdoms in your life. Consider the different ways you learn the important lessons in life and how they change you everyday.

Journal:

1) Have you listened lately? Listen to those around you, listen to yourself and write down the wisdom that you can see in your life today.

2) Think about a teacher, parent, grandparent or friend who says wise things. They can be lessons that you have taken from their teachings, like my mother's wise words.

3) Think about the two words I mentioned in the passage, acceptance and release. How do you see this in your life? Do you hold on to grudges never accepting that it is over and done, then unable to release the feeling so it festers and hurts you not the one it is directed at? Write it all down, release and accept and see what you learn.

Books:

The Prophet by Kahlil Gibran.

The prophet, Almustafa, has lived in the foreign city of Orphalese for 12 years and is about to board a ship that will carry him home. He is stopped by a group of people, with whom he discusses topics such as life and the human condition. The book is divided into chapters dealing with love, marriage, children, giving, eating and drinking, work, joy and sorrow, houses, clothes, buying and selling, crime and punishment, laws, freedom, reason and passion, pain, self-knowledge, teaching, friendship, talking, time, good and evil, prayer, pleasure, beauty, religion, and death.

An Ancient African Wisdom Book by Angela Chamblee

This is an analysis *The Instruction of Ptahhotep*, one of the oldest textbooks on earth; a self-help book, it teaches good manners and ethics and provides advice about how to be successful in life. Aided by illustrations, *An Ancient African Wisdom Book* dissects this eighteen page book of maxims that was written 4,500 years ago and translates these maxims into information that can be applied to life today.

Films:

Gandhi directed by Richard Attenborough starring Ben Kingsley, John Gielgud & Candice Bergman

This is a 1982 biographical film based on the life of Mohandas Karamchand Gandhi, who led the nonviolent resistance movement against British colonial rule in India during the first half of the 20th century. The film was directed and produced by Sir Richard Attenborough and stars Ben Kingsley as Gandhi. They both won Academy Awards for their work on the film. The film was also given the Academy Award for Best Picture and won eight Academy Awards.

Invictus directed by Clint Eastwood starring Morgan Freeman & Matt Damon

On February 2, 1990, Nelson Mandela is released from Victor Verster Prison after 27 years spent in jail. Four years later, Mandela is elected the first black President of South Africa. His presidency faces enormous challenges in the post-Apartheid era, including rampant poverty and crime. Mandela is particularly concerned about racial divisions between black and white South Africans, which could lead to violence. The ill will which both groups hold towards each other, is seen even in his own security detail where relations between the established white officers, who had guarded Mandela's predecessors, and the black ANC additions to the security detail, are frosty and marked by mutual distrust.

While attending a game of the Springboks, the country's rugby union team, Mandela recognizes that the blacks in the stadium cheer against their 'home' squad, as the mostly-white Springboks represent prejudice and apartheid in their minds. He remarks that he did the same while imprisoned on Robben Island. Knowing that South Africa is set to host the 1995 Rugby World Cup in one year's time, Mandela convinces a meeting of the newly black-dominated South African Sports Committee to support the Springboks. He then meets with the captain of the Springboks rugby team, François Pienaar (Matt Damon), and implies that a Springboks victory in the World Cup will unite and inspire the nation. Mandela also shares with Francis a British poem, "Invictus", that had inspired him during his time in prison.

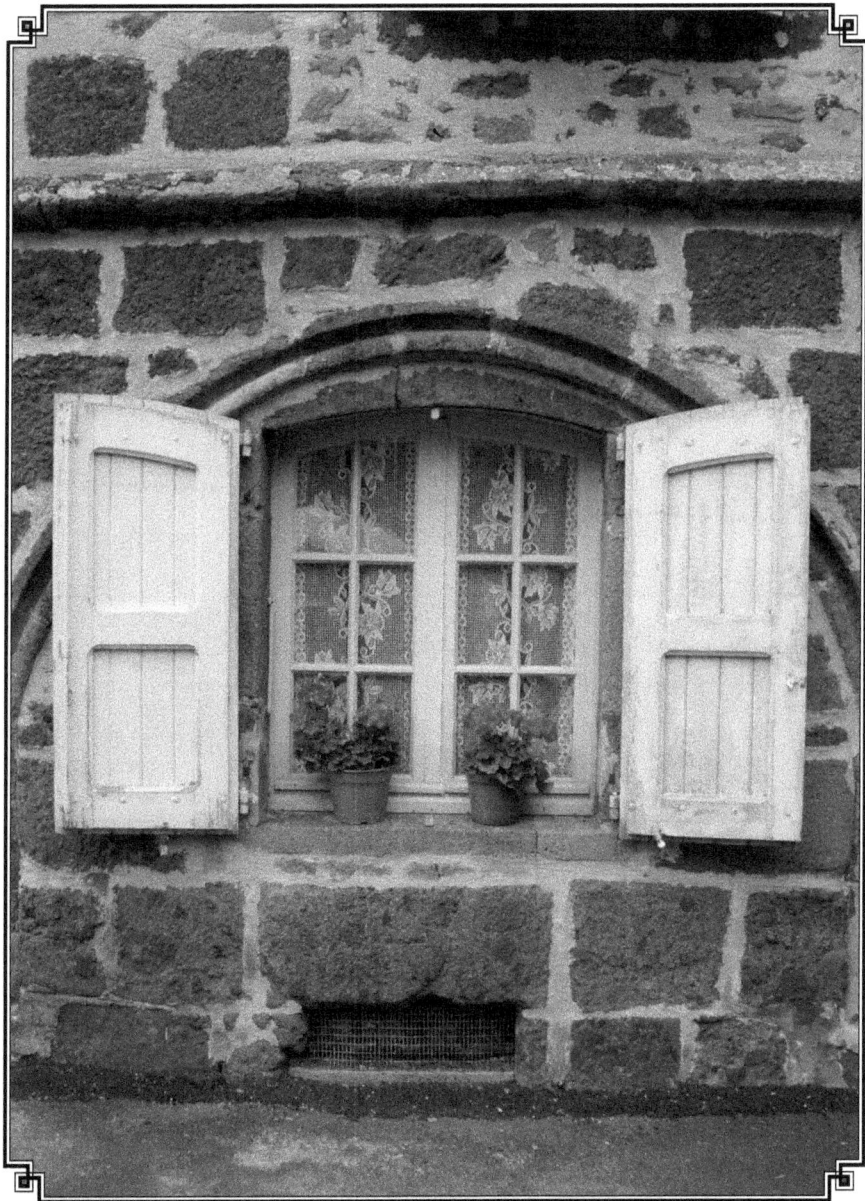

Xenophobia

Xenophobia

Xenophobia is fearing others because they are not us.

Xenophobia is a noun

- an irrational fear of foreigners or strangers.

> As the global expansion of Indian and Chinese restaurants
> suggests, xenophobia is directed against foreign people,
> not foreign cultural imports.
> — E. J. Hobsbawm

EVERY YEAR IN SYNAGOGUE ON THE HIGH HOLIDAYS WE read the word xenophobia. I remember the first time I understood its meaning: "to fear foreigners." I thought about the idea of fearing someone just because they were different from me. My first feeling was sadness because I have been a foreigner in a new world, and the feeling can be frightening.

I was eight years old when I moved from California to England. It was very different from the life I knew. In school the kids were mean, they called me "yank," and I would go home in tears. I discussed my experience with xenophobia in the *Courage* chapter of this book. It was an awful experience but I was taught never to use the word hate. We should not judge others because they are different than we are, and we should not hold those differences against them.

One of the other memories that always stuck with me is that my mom would sing, *You Have to be Taught to Hate* from the musical South Pacific. She would tell my brother and me that hate is taught, and in our home we learned the opposite. We learned to love. I was blessed with my gift of experience and the love of a strong woman who believed we are all created equal. This upbringing made me a social activist, a supporter of Human Rights, and a person determined to stand up for those who cannot stand up for themselves. I feel empowered by my history and am committed to help create a better world for all of us to prosper in.

Today I have great compassion for the foreigner, for the immigrant who speaks a different language, and for the poor person who doesn't belong in the neighborhood. I feel compassion for the child of color who is not allowed to play with others, and the gay person who is beaten because others are disgusted by their existence. Xenophobia is an evil that permeates a society and can destroy it if it is not stopped. It is my belief that we are all human beings on a small planet of infinite energy. Why don't we use the energy for love? We can only evolve if we do it with love. Look at your life, your neighborhood, and our country and honestly ask yourself if you fear the foreigners around you?

This week work to overcome any issues you have against those who are different from you. Focus on how people are similar instead of different and strive to work with individuals you differ from. Working together to end the stigmas of society can enable us to create a global environment in which we all thrive together. Being different should not separate an individual from society; it should distinguish their characteristics from those who surround them.

Journal:

1) Have you ever had a personal experience that could be called xenophobic? Or have you ever seen others around you experience this behavior? If so can you recall it in detail and then re read it with new eyes.

2) Have you ever had the feeling that you fear others because of their difference? This can also be seen as racism, anti Semitism or just plain hate of another group. Many of us have been taught this in our history classes, religious schools or by our families, so write it down and see your reaction to it.

3) Write down all those around you that may have had this experience and talk to them, learn from them, listen to them and then write about what you learn about yourself.

Books:

Hate on the Streets: Xenophobic Violence in Greece by Human Rights Watch

The 99-page report documents the failure of the police and the judiciary to prevent and punish rising attacks on migrants. Despite clear patterns to the violence and evidence that it is increasing, the police have failed to respond effectively to protect victims and hold perpetrators to account, Human Rights Watch found. Authorities have yet to develop a preventive policing strategy, while victims are discouraged from filing official complaints. No one has been convicted under Greece's 2008 hate crime statute.

The Lions of Little Rock by Kristin Levine

Two girls separated by race form an unbreakable bond during the tumultuous integration of Little Rock schools in 1958. Twelve-year-old Marlee doesn't have many friends until she meets Liz, the new girl at school. Liz is bold and brave, and always knows the right thing to say, especially to Sally, the resident mean girl. Liz even helps Marlee overcome her greatest fear - speaking, which Marlee never does outside her family. But then Liz is gone, replaced by the rumor that she was a Negro girl passing as white. But Marlee decides that doesn't matter. Liz is her best friend. And to stay friends, Marlee and Liz are willing to take on integration and the dangers their friendship could bring to both their families.

The Outsiders by S.E. Hinton

Ponyboy, a member of the Greasers gang, is leaving a movie theater when a group of Socs jumps him. His older brothers Darry and Sodapop save him. The next night, Ponyboy and his friends Dally and Johnny meet Cherry Valance and Marcia at a drive-in movie theatre. Ponyboy realizes that Cherry is nothing like the Socs he has met before. The Greasers walk Cherry and Marcia home, and Socs Bob Sheldon and Randy Adderson see them and think the boys are trying to pick up their girlfriends. Cherry and Marcia prevent a fight by leaving with Bob and Randy willingly. When Ponyboy comes home very late, Darry gets angry and hits him. Ponyboy runs away and meets up with Johnny. As they wander around the neighborhood, Bob, Randy, and three other drunken Socs confront them. After a Soc nearly drowns Ponyboy in a fountain, a terrified Johnny stabs Bob, accidentally killing him. Ponyboy and Johnny find Dally, who gives them money and a loaded gun and tells them to hide in an abandoned church. They stay there for a few days, during which time Ponyboy reads *Gone with the Wind* to Johnny and recites the poem "Nothing Gold Can Stay" by Robert Frost.

Shanghi Girls by Lisa See

Shanghai Girls is divided into three parts: Fate, Fortune, and Destiny. It centers on the complex relationship between two sisters, Pearl and May, as they go through great pain and suffering in leaving war-torn Shanghai and try to adjust to the difficult roles of wives in arranged marriages and of Chinese immigrants to the U.S. Here See treats Chinese immigration from a personal view through Pearl's narration. In On Gold Mountain she objectively placed 100 years of her Chinese family history in the context of the daunting challenges Chinese immigrants faced in coming to America in search of Gold Mountain. America's mistreatment of Chinese immigrants is stressed in both memoir and novel. The sisters' story is interrelated with critical historical events, famous people, and important places—the Second Sino-Japanese War, the Battle of Shanghai, internment at Angel Island, Los Angeles Chinatown, Hollywood, World War II, the Chinese Exclusion Act, McCarthyism, etc. Historically significant people appearing in the novel include Madame Chiang Kai-shek, actress Anna May Wong, film personality Tom Gubbins, and Christine Sterling, the "Mother of Olvera Street."

Films:

South Pacific director Josh Logan starring Rossano Brazzi & Mitzi Gaynor

South Pacific is a 1958 musical romance film adaptation of the Rodgers and Hammerstein musical South Pacific, and based on James A. Michener's Tales of the South Pacific. Can a girl from Little Rock find happiness with a mature French planter she got to know one enchanted evening away from the military hospital where she is a nurse? Or should she just wash that man out of her hair? Bloody Mary is the philosopher of the island and it's hard to believe she could be the mother of Liat who has captured the heart of Lt. Joseph Cable USMC. While waiting for action in the war in the South Pacific, sailors and nurses put on a musical comedy show. The war gets closer and the saga of Nellie Forbush and Emile de Becque becomes serious drama.

Gangs of New York directed by Martin Scorsese starring Leonardo DiCaprio, Cameron Diaz & Daniel Day-Lewis

As waves of immigrants swell the population of New York, lawlessness and corruption thrive in Manhattan's Five Points section. After years of incarceration, young Irish immigrant Amsterdam Vallon returns seeking revenge against the rival gang leader who killed his father. But Amsterdam's personal vendetta becomes part of the gang warfare.

Year

Year

Year is a period of time by which we measure our lives.

THE DICTIONARY DEFINITION:

Year is a noun

- a period of time containing 365 (or 366) days; she is 4 years old; in the year 1920; a school year; a Martian year takes 687 of our days;

- a period of time occupying a regular part of a calendar year that is used for some particular activity;

- the period of time that it takes for a planet (as, e.g., Earth or Mars) to make a complete revolution around the sun;

- a body of students who graduate together; the class of '97; she was in my year at Hoehandle High;

> "For last year's words belong to last year's language and next year's words away another voice.".............Little Gidding II
>
> — T.S. Eliot

One year seems to fly by quicker these days than when I was a child. Is it because of computers, jet planes, freeways, and fast food? No, a year goes faster because I am about to turn sixty-two. This year has been an incredible one for me. As I look back at the last twelve months I am in awe of the changes, joys, challenges, adventures, disappointments, and growth that have occurred in my life. When I look at the past, I realize every year is this way. We lose friends and family, enjoy parties and holidays, escape to vacations, and view the miracle of birth. At times, we work hard and make less money than we used to make, or lose the job we thought was secure. Life in one year can change in many ways, especially as we age.

My dear mother put time into perspective for me when she explained that at 80 one year is 1/80 of her life; likewise, my grandson experiences one year as 1/8 of his. This was explained one day in a very visual way that stuck with me. When my grandson, Clovis, said it was a really long time until next summer, my mother explained that life is like a pie. If you cut Clovis' pie into all the years he had lived, there would be 8 pieces, but if you cut the pie into all the years she had lived there would be 80 very small pieces. This is why time seems longer when you are a child and shorter when you are older. As we age we understand the limited amount of time we are given and it is important that each of us make the most of the time we have.

At the beginning of each year I make a vision board and a list of what I want to accomplish that year, but often those things on the list go on to next year's list. For example, this book started twelve years ago on a similar list, and here I am finally finishing it! It is better to start our projects early to accomplish our goals sooner rather than later, and to add new goals to pursue in our lives.

This week put time into perspective. My summary of a year is just a portion of the journey, but remember it is shorter as the years speed by and we grow older. Do what you want now because a year is a gift, every moment is a gift and don't squander any of it.

Journal:

1) What year do you remember best in the past? Was it a year of ups and downs? Write about the things you learned and the experiences you enjoyed.

2) At this time in your life what do you want from the next year? Make a vision board or a list of what you want to accomplish and put it where you can see it every day.

3) Live life to the fullest! Create a twelve-month "joy list". Make a list of 4 things that you want to see or do each month. An exciting, touching, loving, grateful experience that you want to have each week, 52 different acts in one year. There are thousands of opportunities to have a joyful year such as a walk in the woods, painting a picture, making cookies from grandma's cookbook, calling an old friend or playing baseball with the kids down the street. Dream, enjoy and be grateful for the years to come.

Books:

The First Three years of Life by Burton L White

Recognized internationally as one of the most important guides to childhood development ever written, this classic provides the information parents need to maximize a child's social and intellectual potential.

Sikh Festival throughout the Year by Anita Ganeri

Packed with photos, songs and prayers, and fun activities, A Year of Festivals invites readers to join in the festivities of six of the world's major religions. From somber days full of reflection and prayer to parades and parties full of games and dancing, this intriguing series introduces readers to diverse worlds of faith and joy.

Films:

The Best Years of our Lives directed by William Wyler and starring Fredric March, Myrna Loy, Dana Andrews, Teresa Wright, Virginia Mayo, and Harold Russell.

This film is about three United States servicemen trying to piece their lives back together after coming home from World War II. Samuel Goldwyn was inspired to produce a film about veterans after reading an August 7, 1944 article in *Time* about the difficulties experienced by men returning to civilian life. Goldwyn hired former war correspondent MacKinlay Kantor to write a screenplay. His work was first published as a novella, *Glory for Me*, which Kantor wrote in blank verse Robert Sherwood then adapted the novella as a screenplay.

A Year in the Life by Joshua Brand and John Falsey

This was a 1986 Emmy Award–winning miniseries and a one-hour dramatic series that ran on NBC during the 1987–1988 television season, created whose long partnership also produced the television shows *St. Elsewhere, Northern Exposure* and *I'll Fly Away*).

The series began as a three-part miniseries which was first broadcast in December 1986. As suggested by the title, the miniseries followed the various members of the Gardner family of Seattle during the course of one year. The major event of that year was the sudden and unexpected death of wife and mother Ruth Gardner (Eva Marie Saint).

Following the success of the miniseries, NBC decided to launch a one-hour drama series the following fall. Richard Kiley played Joe Gardner, owner of a successful plastics business and father of four adult children. The children were twice-divorced daughter Anne (Wendy Phillips), who had returned home with her two teen-aged children; daughter Lindley (Jayne Atkinson) and husband Jim (Adam Arkin), parents of a newborn baby daughter; black sheep son Jack (Morgan Stevens); and conservative youngest son Sam (David

Oliver), married to free-spirited Kay (Sarah Jessica Parker). Diana Muldaur was a later addition to the cast as Dr. Alice Foley, Joe Gardner's new romantic interest. Trey Ames played Joe Gardner's grandson, David Sisk.

Like Water for Chocolate directed by Alfonso Arau

A film in the style of magical realism based on the popular novel, published in 1989 by first-time Mexican novelist Laura Esquivel. It earned all 11 Ariel awards of the Mexican Academy of Motion Pictures, including the Ariel Award for Best Picture, and became the highest grossing Spanish-language film ever released in the United States at the time.

Early in the film, the audience learns that the protagonist, Tita, is forbidden to marry because of a family tradition. Therefore, when the boy she has been flirting with, Pedro, and his father come to ask for Tita's hand in marriage, Tita's mother, Mama Elena, refuses. Mama Elena offers her other daughter, Rosaura, and Pedro accepts in order to be closer to Tita. Tita bakes the wedding cake with tears causing vomiting, crying, and a longing for their true love in all those who eat it. Mama Elena goes to look at a photo of a man who is later revealed to be her other daughter Gertrudis's true father, news that kills Mama Elena's husband. A year passes and Tita puts her feelings for Pedro in a meal of rose petals. Tita's heat and passion transfers to Gertrudis upon eating the meal. She attempts to cool down by taking a shower, but is overcome with lust and runs off naked with revolutionary soldiers.

Zen

Zen

A light shines from within when one is calm and conscious

THE DICTIONARY DEFINITION
Zen is a noun

- chinese, **Ch'an**. *Buddhism*. a Mahayana movement, introduced into China in the 6th century A.D. and into Japan in the 12th century, that emphasizes enlightenment for the student by the most direct possible means, accepting formal studies and observances only when they form part of such means. Compare <u>koan</u>, <u>mondo.</u>

- the discipline and practice of this sect.

> All that we are is the result of what we have thought. The mind is everything. What we think we become.
>
> — Buddha

When I first wrote the list of words I was going to use in this book, it was going to be for the word "zeal." To have zeal is to have the energy, spirit and enthusiasm to do something. The passion for life is zeal and to create this energy about a subject you feel strongly for can manifest change. When zeal is attributed to a person the word becomes "zealot," which to me means a fanatical person. In my mind the word zealot is negative, for example those who have religious fervor are zealots.

I decided it was not the tone I wish to end this process with, so instead we will work with the word Zen! I think this will help us to become enlightened and not frantic. Hopefully it will give us a sense of peace and love as we complete this six-month process of growth and self-knowledge. Zen is all about wisdom and the attainment of enlightenment. My son, Adam, has been telling the world that he is meditating! He tells them on Facebook how many days he has meditated in a row. I think he is up to 150 now, that is impressive because we all have a number of things to derail us from this practice but by announcing your intention to the world you might have a better chance of attaining the state of Zen!

What is the Meaning of Zen?

Rafael Espericueta captures an accurate description of Zen when he says, "The word Zen has become part of the English language, but what exactly does it mean? It's much easier to answer the question, '*When* is Zen' for that answer would have to be 'Now!'. The whole point of Zen practice is to become fully aware, here and now. To come home to the present moment; this is truly where we live. Thinking verbally takes us far into the past, or into the distant future. But both past and future are fantasies, since the future isn't known and our memories of the past are often quite distorted accounts of what really happened. Zen exhorts one to "Come to your senses!" for when we get lost in thoughts of the past or future, life passes us by. When one mindfully dwells in the present moment, one completely dissolves into whatever activity manifests.

One becomes the activity. Most people have had peak experiences, which all involve being so totally involved with life that one's sense of separateness dissolves into the experience. Very Zen." This week I would like you to think about Zen deeply. As this book comes to a close, reflect on the journey of these past few weeks. Live in the moment of all your experiences and learn to let go of the past. By doing so, you can move forward in your life and take a step closer to the person you want to become.

Journal:

1) When are you feeling the moment? Do you meditate? If not check out Transcendental Meditation it's not spiritual but it will help you to be in the moment. (www.tm.org)

2) Sit down and eat a piece of chocolate or an apple. Eat it with all the presence you can find. Taste it, smell it, chew it, swallow it, feel every sensation and then write about it. See what you learn about the act of eating.

3) Breathe...slowly breathe in on a count of five then hold for a count of five then release for a count of five. Do this practice five times and then write your awareness of your breath, your lungs, and your heart.

Books:

**The TM Book: How to enjoy the rest of your Life
by Denise Denniston Ph.D**

This delightful best seller long a favorite for introducing the Transcendental Meditation program to friends, is updated with 80 new pages covering TH-Sidhi program, the Maharishi Vedic Approach to health programs and the Unified Field of Natural Law.

Zen and the Art of Motorcycle Maintenance: An Inquiry into Values by Robert M. Pirsig

(ZAMM) is a 1974 philosophical novel, the first of Robert M. Pirsig's a text in which he explores his Metaphysics of Quality? The book sold 5 million copies worldwide. It was originally rejected by 121 publishers, more than any other bestselling book, according to the *Guinness Book of Records*. The title is an apparent play on the title of the book *Zen in the Art of Archery* by Eugen Herrigel. In its introduction, Pirsig explains that, despite its title, "it should in no way be associated with that great body of factual information relating to orthodox Zen Buddhist practice. It's not very factual on motorcycles, either."

Films:

A Walk of Wisdom by Victoria Holt

In this intimate and moving portrait we take a Walk of Wisdom with Mae Chee Sansanee Sthirasuta, the revered female spiritual leader of Thailand. For the first time, this compassionate Buddhist nun shares her life, her work and wisdoms and takes us on a breathtaking journey from her former days as a top model to her every day of helping others and living a life of peace and true beauty that really does come from the heart.

Zen: The Best of Alan Watts

A person who thinks all the time has nothing to think about except faults, so he loses touch with reality and lives in a world of illusions. By thought I mean the chattering inside the skull, perpetual and compulsive repetition of words, of calculations, and symbols going on inside the head. For as a result of confusing the real world of nature with mere signs, such as money, stocks and bonds, title deeds, and so forth. This is a disaster. Time to wake up. Alan Watts (1915-1973) who held both a master's degree in theology and a doctorate of divinity, is best known as an interpreter of Zen Buddhism in particular, and Indian and Chinese philosophy in general. He authored more than 20 excellent books on the philosophy and psychology of religion, and lectured extensively, leaving behind a vast audio archive. With characteristic lucidity and humor Watts unravels the most obscure ontological and epistemological knots with the greatest of ease.

Books & Films

It has been a pleasure to compile this series of books and films with the help of the Internet especially Wikipedia and IMDI.

Attitude

- Think and Grow Rich by Napoleon Hill
- The Power of Positive Thinking by Norman Vincent
- *Life is Beautiful with Roberto Benigni*
- *A Beautiful Mind with Russell Crowe*
- *Robot and Frank*

Beauty

- Sophia Loren's Recipes and Memories by Sophia Loren
- How, then, Shall We Live? Four Simple Questions that Reveal the Beauty and Meaning in Our Lives by Wayne Muller
- *Mask with Cher*
- *On Beauty, directed by Joanna Rudnick (In the Family)*

Courage

- What Color is your Parachute? By Richard Nelson Bolles
- One Thousand White Women by Jim Fergus
- The Aladdin Factor by Jack Canfield and Mark Victor Hansen
- *Julia with Jane Fonda and Vanessa Redgrave*
- *Milk with Sean Penn & Josh Brolin*
- *Man of La Mancha by Dale Wasserman*

Discipline

- The Fifth Discipline: The Art and Practice of the Learning Organization by Peter Senge
- Celebrating discipline: the path to spiritual growth By Richard J. Foster
- *Apollo 13 director Ron Howard starring Tom Hanks & Kevin Bacon*
- *Karate Kid Directed by John G. Avildsen with Ralph Macchio, Pat Morita and Elisabeth Shue*
- *Harts War(directed Gregory Hoblit starring Bruce Willis & Colin Farrell*

Environment

- Bounded people, boundless land by Eric T. Freyfogel
- The western guide to Feng Shui – by Terah Kathryn Collins
- *Baraka by Ron Fricke*
- *Taken for a Ride by Martha Olson*
- *Fuel directed by Josh Tickell.*

Focus

- "The Power of Focus" Jack Canfield, MV Hansen & Les Hewitt
- "Manifest Your Destiny" by Wayne Dyer
- *Million Dollar Baby Directed by Clint Eastwood*
- *Hugo is a 2011 American 3D adventure drama film*

Giving

- 'The Giving Tree' by Shel Silverberg
- Authors Harvey McKinnon & Azim Jamal
- *Aemelie: (Audrey Tautou)*
- *The Soloist: The film is based on a true story of Nathaniel Ayers*
- *Magnificent Obsession directed by Douglas Sirk*

Health

- Deepak Chopra, M.D is the author of more than 65 books,
- You Being Beautiful, by Drs. Oz and Roizen.
- Anatomy of an Illness by Norman Cousins
- *50/50 by Jonathan Levine*
- *Supersize Me by Morgan Spurlock*

Intimacy

- Intimate Connections by David Burns
- The Dance of Intimacy by Harriet Learner
- *The Waking Life by Richard Linklater*
- *Garden State written, directed and starring Zach Braff,*
- *Casablanca directed by Michael Curtiz,*

Journey

- December Sky: Beyond My Undocumented Life by Evelyn Cortez-Davis
- A Road Less Travelled by M. Scott Peck
- No-No Boy by John Okada
- *Homeless to Harvard*
- *127 Hours by Danny Boyle*

Knowledge

- Holler If You Hear Me: Searching for Tupac Shakur by Michael Eric Dyson
- Dictionary of Cultural Literacy: What Every American Needs to Know

- Atlas Shrugged is a novel by Ayn Rand
- *Good Will Hunting Starring Matt Damon, Robin Williams, Ben Affleck*
- *Crash directed by Paul Haggis*

Laughter

- Junie B. Jones series by Barbara Parker
- Dress Your Family in Corduroy and Denim by David Sedaris
- *Patch Adams with Robin Williams directed by Tom Shadyac*
- *Mr. Bean's Holiday with Rowan Atkinson directed by Steve Bendelack*
- *Blazing Saddles directed by Mel Brooks*

Money

- The Soul of Money by Lynne Twist
- First Comes Love then comes Money by Bethany & Scott Palmer
- The Richest Man in Babylon by George Samuel Clason
- The Money Book for the Young, Fabulous & Broke by Suze Orman
- The Complete Idiot's Guide to Managing Your Money, 4th Edition
- *Money Ball. By Bennett Miller with Brad Pitt & Robin Wright*
- *Wall Street directed by Oliver Stone with Michael Douglas, Charlie Sheen*
- *The Corporation by Mark Achbar, Jennifer Abbott & Joel Bakan*

Nature

- Silent Spring by Rachel Carson
- Earth Odyssey by Michael Hertsgaard
- *Oceans by Jacques Perrin*
- *Ferngully: The Last Rainforest directed by Bill Kroyer with Samantha Mathis, Christian Slater.*
- *March of the Penguins directed by Luc Jacquet. with Morgan Freeman, Charles Berling.*

Oneness

- Leviathan written by Thomas Hobbes
- Walden written by Henry David Thoreau.
- Of The Social Contract, Principles of Political Right by Jean-Jacques Rousseau,
- *I AM directed by Tom Shadyac*
- *The Celestine Prophecy by James Redfield*

Passion

- The Agony and the Ecstasy: A Novel of Michelangelo
- My Life in France is an autobiography by Julia Child
- *Pride and Predudice by Jane Austin screenplay Deborah Moggach, director Joe Wright starring Keira Knightly*
- *Under the Tuscan Sun directed by Audrey Wells starring Diane Lane*
- *Midnight in Paris directed and written by : Woody Allen Stars: Owen Wilson, Rachel McAdams and Kathy Bates*
- *The Aviator directed by Martin Scorsese, written by John Logan, starring Leonardo DiCaprio*

Quality

- Yesterday, I Cried : Celebrating the Lessons of Living and Loving by Iyanla Vanzant
- Lean Forward into Your Life: Begin Each Day As If It Were on Purpose By Mary Anne Radmacher
- The Invitation author Oriah Mountain Dreamer
- *Gia starring Angelina Jolie*
- *It's a Wonderful Life produced and directed by Frank Capra*
- *The Fountainhead director King Vidor starring Gary Cooper & Patricia Neal*

Response

- The Choice by Eliyahu M. Goldratt
- The Seven Habits of Hightly Effective People by Stephen Covey

- *The Help Directed by Tate Taylor. Starring Emma Stone, Viola Davis.*
- *Slumdog Millionaire directed by Danny Boyle, written by Simon Beaufoy*

Spirit

- Man's Quest for God by Abraham Heschel
- Autobiography of a Yogi by Paramahansa Yogananda
- Toward a True Kinship of Faiths by His Holiness the Dalai Lama
- Rumi: a spiritual biography
- *What the Bleep Do We Know! Director William Arntz, Betsy Chasse & Mark Vicente starring Marlee Matlin*
- *The Shawshank Redemption written and directed by Frank Darabont and starring Tim Robbins and Morgan Freeman.*
- *A Walk of Wisdom written and directed by Victoria Holt*
- *Finding Neverland starring Johnny Depp and Kate Winslet*

Talent

- The Talent Code by Daniel Coyle
- Monograph by Diane Arbus
- *August Rush directed by Kirsten Sheridan starring Freddie Highmore & Keri Russell*
- *Bagdad Café - directed by Percy Adlon*

Unconditional

- America is in the Heart – an autobiography by Carlos Bulosan
- The Four Loves by C. S. Lewis
- *Ladder 49 – directed by Jay Russell starring Joaquin Phoenix & John Travolta*
- *Man on Fire – directed by Tony Scott starring Denzel Washington & Dakota Fanning*

Vision

- The Vision Board: The Secret to an Extraordinary Life by Joyce Schwarz
- Life Visioning: A Transformative Process for Activating Your Unique Gifts and Highest Potential by Michael Bernard Beckwith
- Living the Life of Your Dreams by Marilyn Tam
- Anne Franks Diary
- *The Secret directed by Drew Heriot Produced by Rhonda Byrne*
- *Rudy: directed by David Anspaugh written by Angelo Pizzo*
- *The Diary of Anne Frank by George Stevens*
- *Gandhi by Richard Attenborough*

Wisdom

- The Profit by Kahlil Gibran
- An Ancient African Wisdom Book, author Angela Chamblee
- Tuesdays With Morrie by Mitch Albon
- The Giver by Lois Lowry
- *Invictus directed by Clint Eastwood starring Morgan Freeman & Matt Damon*
- *Raising Victor Vargas directed by Peter Sollett,*
- *Coach Carter directed by Thomas Carter starring Samuel L Jackson & Rick Gonzalez*

Xenophobia

- Hate on the Streets: Xenophobic Violence in Greece by Human Rights Watch
- The Lions of Little Rock by Kristin Levine
- The Outsiders by S. E. Hinton
- Shanghi Girls by Lisa See
- *South Pacific directed Joshua Logan starring Mitzi Gaynor, Rossano Brazzi*
- *Gangs of New York directed by Martin Scorsese starring Daniel Day Lewis Cameron Diaz Leonardo DiCaoril*

- *Elf directed by Jon Favreau starring Will Ferrell & Bob Newhart*

Year

- The First Three years of Life by Burton L White
- Like Water for Chocolate by Laura Esquivel
- Sikh Festival throughout the Year by Anita Ganeri
- A Year By the Sea by Joan Anderson (Y)
- *The Best Years of Our Lives directed by William Wyler starring Fredric March, Myrna Loy, Dana Andrews*
- *A Year in the Life created by Joshua Brand and John Falsey*
- *Freedom Riders by historian Raymond Arsenault. Directed by Stanley Nelson,*
- *One Day directed by Lone Scherfig starring Anne Hathaway Jim Sturgess*

Zen

- The TM Book: How to enjoy the rest of your Life By Denise Denniston Ph.D
- Zen and the Art of Motorcycle Maintenance: An Inquiry into Values by Robert M. Pirsig
- *A Walk of Wisdom by Victoria Holt*
- *Zen: The Best of Alan Watts*

Acknowledgements

I worked with young women interns from UCSB to help me create an up to date library for all to enjoy and an edited version of my words. Thank you so much Anita Tokatyan and Anna Amirkhanian-Haftvani. Kathy Winter helped me to create the beautiful cover art for this book and I will be forever grateful, as it is exactly what I had envisioned. My dear friend and "adopted sister" Sue Colin helped in the editing and with the manifestation of this project with her support, encouragement and much more! In addition my ninety-three year old mother, Sheila Ehrman, was asked to give input and was the one with great insight and ideas into the films and books that were chosen, she was my first editor! I am dyslexic and she is an editor, go figure! Thank you all for making this book possible.

Anita Tokatyan is a first-generation Armenian-American student at the University of California, Santa Barbara. She was born in Southern California and enrolled in the university after graduating high school. She is currently studying in the English department and is pursuing a minor in professional writing. Anita's passion for writing developed at a young age when she was introduced to the world of imagination through literature. Her love to read and write grew over the years and she plans to continue her studies in literature. She hopes her experience with *Portals of Life* is only the beginning of her writing career.

Anna Amirkhanian-Haftvani was born and raised in Southern California in an Armenian household. She attended primary and secondary school in the Glendale Unified School District, and then enrolled at the University of California Santa Barbara in the fall of 2009. At UCSB. In the summer of 2012, Anna interned for the non-profit organization, Human Rights Watch. She plans to spend a semester studying in Washington D.C. during her senior year as an undergraduate. She expects to receive her Bachelor of Arts degree in Political Science in 2013, and teach English abroad before attending graduate school.

The Portals of Life can be studied with the author weekly thru her online webinars. Check for available times and days at www.theportalsoflife.com7

www.ingramcontent.com/pod-product-compliance
Lightning Source LLC
Chambersburg PA
CBHW062213080426
42734CB00010B/1871